THREE NIGHTS
at the Condor

THREE NIGHTS
at the Condor

A Coal Miner's Son, Carol Doda, and the Topless Revolution

Benita Mattioli

Keisho Publications

*Dedicated to Phyllis and Clyde Christensen
and Elena and Pietro Mattioli.*

PHOTO CREDITS

pp. x, 19, 21, 30, 132, 165, 187, 191, 192, 210, 215, 231, 238, 239, 240
© 2018 Benita and Pete Mattioli.

p. 101 © Gordon Peters / San Francisco Chronicle / Polaris; p. 137 © Mike Alexander / San Francisco Chronicle / Polaris; p. 234 © Paul Chinn / San Francisco Chronicle / Polaris; p. 237 © Eric Luse / San Francisco Chronicle / Polaris.

Fang family San Francisco Examiner photograph archive photographic negative files, BANC PIC 2006.029: [139459_06_05–NEG (p. 93), 139459_l 3_10–NEG (p. 115), 139459¬_10_08–NEG (p. 120), 139459_10_11–NEG (p. 122), 139459_12_01–NEG (p. 138), 139459_17_02–NEG (p. 141), 139460D_02_11–NEG (p. 156), 142247_01_26–NEG (p. 182), 142247_01_08–NEG (p. 183)], Box 1458. © The Regents of the University of California, The Bancroft Library, University of California, Berkeley.

p. 142 © Bettmann/Getty Images; p. 177 © Tim Boxer/Getty Images.

p. 210 © 1973 June Fallaw.

ISBN 978-0-578-41667-0

10 9 8 7 6 5 4 3 2

Contents

Pete at age 16.

Introduction

Since I came into Pete Mattioli's life in 1970 (and married him eleven years later), I experienced many of the happenings recorded in this book. I met Carol Doda on several occasions, and found her to be very charming. I also knew many of the other characters of North Beach, including Gino Del Prete, Davey Rosenberg, Lucky Lucchessi, Coke Infante, Pee Wee Ferrari, Art Thanish, Maurice Bessiere and Jimmy "The Beard" Ferrozzo. I became friends with several of these people— and some scared me to death.

I've heard these stories over and over at the hundreds of dinners we've hosted, and through visiting with people who were in North Beach during the 1960s and 1970s. It was such a special time in The City, and I've always known that these stories must be told.

In 1958, Pete became a partner with Gino Del Prete in The Condor nightclub. The evolution of the club into becoming the first topless bar in the United States is carefully detailed in this book. At first, it was just an ordinary neighborhood bar with a jukebox—but Pete and Gino had an-other vision for it. During the early 1960s, they remodeled, enlarging the club, and booked rock'n'roll groups. One of the groups, George and Teddy and the Condors, was instrumental in the success of the club during that time. They were so popular, in fact, that when they were on tour in Rome, the Beatles came to see *them*! (See Chapter Nine.) Pete also hired Davey Rosenberg, who carried out all kinds of promotional gimmicks to bring crowds into the Condor.

Pete hired Carol Doda, a pretty young lady, as a cocktail waitress. She had a lovely figure, but it was not extraordinary in any way. Carol was coaxed into dancing on the bar, and then into dancing on the piano played by a popular entertainer named Billy Dare. She wore her cocktail outfit, black leotards and a white body suit. On June 19, 1964, when Carol first wore the "topless swimsuit" in her act, she was still an A-cup size on top; nevertheless, it has become known as the first shot fired in the "Topless Revolution."

Through the years, I've heard astonishing rumors, often inaccurate, about these times. I've thought it important that someone who was actually there (Pete) tell his stories as he experienced the events. One speculation I wanted to put to rest was that Pete had a Mafia connection, due to his Italian name and nightclub ownership. Nothing could be further from the truth. He was a coal miner's son.

The book's title alludes to the 1975 Robert Redford/Faye Dunaway movie *Three Days of the Condor*, and I have highlighted the three nights everyone thinks of when they think of the Condor nightclub: the night Carol first went topless, the night she got busted, and the night Jimmy the Beard died on top of the piano.

This is my first book and it has taken me ten years to put together. I knew I had to do extensive research and get all the facts correct. This is the true story of the two wildly ambitious North Beach Italians who owned the Condor, and the quest for fame of the beautiful, the one and only, Carol Doda.

1

Coal Country

Pietro Mattioli, Pete's father, set sail from Naples, Italy, on board the *Ancona* in early September, 1914. He had said good-bye to his mama and papa back home in Sassoferrato, promising he would write. Cousin Giovanni Vittiletti, who lived in Peckville, Pennsylvania, had written that Pietro could get a job in the coal mines outside of Peckville, a small village of 1,500 or so people, located along the banks of the Lackawanna River about ten miles northeast of Scranton, in the northeast section of Pennsylvania's rich anthracite coal basin. Pietro, a strong sixteen-year-old, planned to make lots of money, marry, and get out of the coal mines as soon as he could. When the ship docked in New York harbor one month later, he and many of the Italian passengers traveled to Pennsylvania by train.

Most of the immigrant families in the area were of Italian, Polish, German, or Russian descent. As did many of the single male settlers, Pietro moved into a boarding house and was quickly hired by the mine foreman. Strong young men were needed for the grueling and hazardous job of mining the high-quality hard anthracite coal more than 300 feet below the surface.

The minimum age to work in the mines was fourteen. Many parents lied and stated their son was just small for his age. Some of the boys were as young as ten. The most common job for the boys was breaking and sorting coal in the colliery. The "breaker boys" sat on wooden planks as the coal moved through chutes under them. They used their feet to slow or stop the coal as they picked out rocks and other debris and threw them in a pile. There were no backrests, and the boss wouldn't let them wear gloves, as they had a better feel for the coal without them. The noise from the machinery was earsplitting, and their bodies ached after working 12-hour shifts on the breaker lines.

Some boys were employed at the door openings as "nippers," responsible for opening and closing the heavy wooden doors for the loaded rail cars to proceed through. The doors were a critical part of the ventilation system and needed to be closed unless a coal car was coming through. If the boys were not paying attention or if they fell asleep, the fast moving coal carts would slam through the doors with disastrous results: the boys could be pinned against the walls or run over by the coal car.

The quickest and most nimble boys were used as "spraggers." Their job was to slow the speed of coal cars by running alongside them, jamming pieces of wood through the wheels. Many young boys lost their fingers or feet, or were killed performing this extremely dangerous job.

The air quality down in the caves was so unhealthy the miners wore bandanas in an attempt to filter out the coal dust. Rat colonies populated the mines, and were always waiting for a tiny scrap of a miner's lunch to be left behind. Cave-ins were also common, but casualties were infrequent; nevertheless, the danger was always there.

Despite harsh working conditions and long hours, the boys of the coal mines kept their spirits up by teasing and playing jokes on each other. If they had a chance and the boss wasn't looking, they might "unintentionally" break a critical piece of machinery, which would stop the whole operation. That meant some serious playtime for the boys.

As a way to make extra income, many families in the area housed and fed single coal miners; the boarders paid a few dollars each month for a bed, meals, and laundry services. One such house was run by Lucia and Giovanni Furiosi, who had immigrated to the States early in their marriage, and all of whose seven children—Elena, Mary, Lizzy, Gino, Johnny, Dante, and Peter—were born in the United States. The large home they owned on Maple Street in the center of town was actually two homes in one. It was divided—or connected, depending upon which way you wanted to characterize it—by a swinging door. Each section of the house had a complete kitchen and several bedrooms. The home had a large covered porch, which wrapped around all four sides of the house.

When Pietro was twenty-four, he moved into the Furiosi home, becoming one of four men who received a bed and meals from the family. It wasn't long before he had caught the eye of Elena, the sweet fourteen-year-old daughter of Lucia and Giovanni, who had a shy giggle but a lively sense of humor. Because Pietro was ten years her senior, he had to wait for her to grow up. When Elena was sixteen, Pietro proposed, and they were married that same year. Their wedding portrait reveals a standing Pietro by the side of a sitting Elena, so petite that she requested a pillow be placed under her feet to create the impression that she was much more mature.

Once married, Pietro and Elena moved into one side of the house and began a family. Elena's father had passed away by then, so her mother, Lucia, and her single sons, Gino, Johnny, and Danny, occupied the other side of the home. (Mary and Lizzy soon were married and moved into homes of their own; the other sons, Peter and Angelo, had also moved on with their lives.)

Elena gave birth to all her children at home. Although there were plenty of women around to help with the birthing, a midwife was often called to document the births. Families and neighbors tended to each other's needs, whether it was a birth, an injury, sickness, or any other crisis. They shared each other's sorrows and celebrated the happy times as well. Births were always joyous occasions.

The women's daily lives were entwined, sharing their work, hopes, dreams, and secrets, trading recipes and listening to radio broadcasts. Cooking, cleaning, and household chores made up most of the day for the women who worked in the home. They made lots of pasta. Beginning with a mountain of flour placed in the middle of the table, they would carve a hole into the center of the mound and crack several eggs into it. By hand, the flour was gradually introduced to the eggs, and the kneading began. After rolling the dough into thin sheets on a wooden board, they would fashion it into differently shaped pastas: tagliatelle, spaghetti, and tortellini. Ravioli was made by rolling out a big sheet of pasta, placing the spinach and meat filling in rows, and folding a layer of pasta over the top. Individual ravioli were cut with a knife and closed on the edges with a fork. The pasta was then dried on a bedsheet placed over the table. (In "Lazy Mary," a popular Italian song recorded by Louis Prima, and heard at the wedding in *The Godfather*, he sings, "Lazy Mary, you'd better get up. We need the sheets for the table.")

Textile companies saw the opportunity to locate manufacturing to the coal mining areas to take advantage of the cheap labor available. Hundreds of women seeking to add to the family income were employed by the silk and lace mills. Pietro's brother Archangelo's wife, Lisa, worked as a seamstress in one of these mills.

The men of Peckville were all hunters. The annual deer hunt was so anticipated it was talked about all throughout the year. Local deer were abundant, and the hunt was a time-honored tradition. During the season, the deer that were shot legitimately and tagged hung like trophies in front of most of the homes. The deer that were killed without a tag were hidden in garages and outbuildings around town.

Pietro often brought home rabbit, quail, squirrel, and pheasant to be prepared and shared at the dinner table. He would often give his children the tails of such animals, which they considered good luck. The women came up with delicious sauces for the wild game using whatever was available, usually featuring onions, garlic, parsley, tomatoes, rosemary, and other herbs. They sometimes added vinegar to the sauces, which diminished the wild taste of the meat. The wild game dishes were often served atop a bed of soft polenta. Whatever they prepared tasted good to the hungry coal miners, and coming home to a delicious hot meal was one of the few pleasures in their dull lives.

The men toiled in the mines, picking and shoveling coal from dusk to dark. Pietro was promoted to mine foreman; however, he continued to work deep in the mines alongside the other miners. He was highly respected by the workers for his insistence that all safety rules be followed. His crew would become angry when asked to "Shore it up! Do it again! I want it right!" He kept his crews safe and prevented many cave-ins by making his men adhere to the rules.

Pietro and Elena's first child, a daughter, was named Francine. In 1926, their first son, Angelo, was born, followed by Pete and Elaine. At the age of seven, Francie became very ill and was diagnosed with spinal meningitis. She passed away shortly afterward, a devastating loss for the young family.

Pete attended Lincoln Grade School in Peckville, which included grades one through eight. Pete was a little guy and wanted to follow his brother and cousins everywhere they went; it seemed like they could never ditch him. He wanted to be sure he didn't miss any of the excitement around town.

His home was adjacent to a road that the high school athletic teams used in their training program. Uncle Gino was a star football player at Blakley, and Pete knew the approximate time and day that the team would run by his home. He was always there to cheer him on, dreaming of the day when he himself would be on the football team.

The family carried on the Italian Old World tradition of meat processing and curing in Peckville. When the family procured a pig, it would be processed in the basement. Every part of the pig was used, turned into ham, bacon, coppa, prosciutto, salami, sausage, mortadella, or porchetta. For making sausage, they fed ground parts of the pig into a hand-operated meat-grinder, which funneled the pork into the skins of the intestines. The meats were oiled and hung on twine ropes from the ceiling of the basement beams of the home.

A small creek behind their home fed into the Lackawanna River, and with the spring snowmelt, the creek would flood into downtown Peckville. From time to time, floodwaters would engulf the basement of the Furiosi home, which was used to store coal and house the home-made cured meats. A frantic effort would then be made to move the coal out of the basement to higher ground and pump out the water. At times when the basement was flooded and Pietro wanted to retrieve one of his hanging meats, he would call on his youngest and lightest son, Pete. Pete would scramble into an aluminum tub attached to a rope and float him out into the room, where his dad would point to the cured meats he wanted. With a knife, Pete would cut the attached line, grab the meat, and his dad would pull the tub back to him.

Pete's childhood was full of friends and family. He had a paper route and borrowed his brother Angelo's bike for deliveries. He had many chores, including shoveling snow from the walkways and the dirt road in front of the house. A group of kids in the neighborhood found an old toboggan that they would pull to the top of Maple Street, which had several dips coming down the hill. They piled up to ten kids on it and rode it over the snow-packed road down what they called the "loop-de-loops."

The family was poor, and Pete remembers waiting in line to buy potatoes and shoes. They didn't have a phone in the house, but the two "old maids" who lived across the street did. If Pete's family needed to make a call, the ladies allowed them to use their phone, and called to them from across the street when they received a call for the Mattiolis.

Pete was a big-time dreamer. His bedroom was upstairs in the home, and on hot summer nights he would open the window for some fresh air and wonder about what the future held for him. He could hear laughter from the nearby beer garden and organ music being played in the roller skating rink a block away. He sometimes peeked through the rink windows, where he could see the town showoff, Alfred Alimenti, scooping up a pretty girl and twirling her above his head while gliding smoothly around the rink. Alfred's biggest trick was to place a match in the girl's mouth and spin her down to light it on the floor. Alfred later married Nancy, Aunt Mary's daughter.

Pete was constantly pushing the limits of discipline with his parents even though he felt his dad had a special fondness for him. He recalls how his mother used to spank him a few times before heading out to church on Sunday or any special gathering. Pete's cries of "What was that for? What did I do?" were usually answered by "That's not for what you've done. That's for what you're gonna do."

There was plenty of racism within the coal communities. Besides the Italians, there were many Polish, Russian, and Irish families. It seemed like all the East Coast hated the Irish. The Irish were the cops and they looked down on the Italians, whom they called wops, guineas, or dagos. It was rumored that all Italians were involved with the Mafia. Pete later recalled his dad saying, "At three dollars a day, how is it that they think I'm in the damned Mafia?" Being associated with the Mafia was something many Italian-Americans had to constantly deny, which is still somewhat true today.

One day, Pete was just hanging around with the big boys when his Uncle Gino and Alfred decided to climb the cherry tree in their backyard to pick the recently ripened fruit. Pete was underneath the tree catching the cherries in his shirt and placing them in a bucket as they were tossed down to him. Suddenly they heard a loud crack. The large branch the men were standing on broke and fell to the ground, trapping Pete underneath and breaking his leg.

Gino and Alfred carried Pete to the hospital, where his leg was placed in a cast, then disappeared for a week. The family didn't have any money to pay the bill. Pietro paid some, but when the hospital found out he had $300 in the bank, his entire savings, it was able to withdraw the full amount to pay the bill. The coal mining companies were very powerful in these small towns, and if the hospital requested help in securing payment, the coal bosses would call the bankers and get the payment. Whatever the coal mining company bosses wanted was pretty much what they got.

On a hot summer day Pietro decided to take his sons into the mines. Pete was flabbergasted at what he saw. It was very dark, dirty, cool, and wet. The mine had its own musty smell, and the air seemed thick. He saw the caged canaries and mules that spent most of their lives inside the mines and only came up when they were too old, blind, or injured to complete their tasks. He felt sorry for them.

Whenever the sirens rang out in Peckville, fear struck, and everyone dropped what he or she was doing and ran straight to the mines. If there was a problem at one of the mines, it was quite possible that someone you knew was in grave danger. Families would gather as close to the mine entrance as was allowed and wait for word about their men or boys. A pipe would be driven through the cave to give the miners air.

Angelo and Pete were sent out almost daily to scavenge coal from the culm banks, loose piles of coal that had already been through the breaker process but still held small chips of coal. The boys would put coal chips into a gunnysack and bring it home to supplement the coal their parents had purchased. Scavenging coal from the culm banks was illegal since they were also owned by the mine companies, and if you were caught your family could face a fine. Pete recalls that, "If the old man said go get coal, you went and got coal."

Beginning in the 1920s and 1930s, coal was becoming less and less popular as a source of heat for homes and power for equipment. Coal was dirty, difficult to harvest, and expensive to transport. Oil, gas, and electricity were much cleaner and becoming more widely available. The anthracite coal of the region was rapidly becoming obsolete. Pietro felt that his health was deteriorating due to coal dust particles; he had begun coughing them up, and had several small chunks of coal embedded in his face and body from blasts within the mine. He was absolutely determined that his boys would not have to work in the coal mines.

Two of Elena's sisters had moved to San Francisco and had often spoken of their desire to have the entire family move to California. Elena had received postcards from California showing beautiful beaches, palm trees, and sun-kissed bathing beauties. Pete took one postcard to school in Peckville to show his teacher just what his new life would be like if his dad moved the family there. They had also heard stories of men discovering gold in California. He was told that everybody was rich in California.

World War II had begun, and Pietro knew there were plenty of jobs in California. He made his decision. He would move his family to California. Irresistible California.

2

No Beach in North Beach?

A crimson droplet splashed on Pete's arm, waking him from a restless sleep. The rumbling noise reminded him that he was still on the train. The pungent odor of alcohol filled the air as the train rolled on through the mountain moonlight. Looking up, he could see the red drops were coming from their bags, which were tucked in the compartment above them. He nudged his mother's arm to wake her and pointed to the bin above them.

"Look, Mom," he said with concern.

"*O Dio cane*," Elena exclaimed. She jumped up and pulled the bag down from the compartment. A wine bottle had broken inside the bag, saturating their belongings, staining their most important personal documents, birth and baptismal certificates, etc. Worse than that, they wouldn't be able to deliver the wine to Pietro in San Francisco. Pete's father would be very disappointed, as he had worked so hard to make that wine, and considered it very special.

They had departed Scranton, Pennsylvania, three days earlier and would soon be in sunny California. Their destination was the idealistic sounding 22 Cadell Place, home of Aunt Mary and Uncle "Toe-to-Toe." (His real name was Angelo, but when he was a child, his sister couldn't pronounce it, so she called him "Toe-to-Toe"; the name stuck.)

Though she was only two, Elaine was trying her best to help her mother clean up the wine mess, carefully removing items from the bag, one by one. They patted them with toilet paper from the lavatory. "This stinks, Mom," Pete retorted, showing his frustration with the embarrassing situation. He had been told it was going to take a long time to get to San Francisco, but he figured it had been long enough, and was getting anxious to arrive. A porter came along and asked if they needed any help. Elena refused the offer, but Pete wished she had accepted. He liked the porters on the train. He felt important when his Mom gave him ten cents or a quarter to tip them. Pete was only eleven, but he wanted to show that he was capable of taking care of business.

Elaine began to cry. She was hungry, irritated, and bursting with the uncontrolled energy of a confined two-year-old.

"Here, sweetie," Elena responded, offering her some coppa and bread from their food bag, which after three days on the train smelled very pungent. Pete was somewhat embarrassed whenever his mom opened it up, but they couldn't afford the luxury of eating in the dining car.

Looking out the window the next morning, Pete noticed they were crossing a body of water. People were swimming and floating in the water alongside the tracks. Some were waving as the train passed, so Elaine and Pete excitedly waved back. Pete exclaimed, "Mom, look, it's the ocean!"

"I don't think so, darling," Elena explained. "I think it is the Great Salt Lake." Disappointed, Pete prepared himself for another day on the train.

The next day, the train slowly rolled into the station by the Oakland Pier at the bottom of 7th Street. The railroad also owned the ferry services to San Francisco, so a smooth connection was made. The San Francisco–Oakland Bay Bridge had been completed six years earlier and did have rail service across it, part of the Key System built to serve Bay Area commuters. (The Key System later became Bay Area Rapid Transit and AC Transit.)

The excitement of the weary travelers was somewhat dampened due to the dark and dreary day filled with heavy rain and strong winds. The family gathered their belongings and transferred to a ferry to make the Bay crossing. They tried their best to keep their belongings dry. As the ferry crossed the Bay, the travelers marveled at the Bay Bridge, a wonder of engineering and the longest steel structure in the world at that time.

Pietro and his eldest son, Angelo, were already in San Francisco, having arrived earlier in the year to look for a job. They had been living with Mary, Elena's sister, and her husband, Toe-to-Toe, in a flat in North Beach. It was the spring of 1942, and the United States was gearing up to go to war with Japan after the bombing of Pearl Harbor in December. Jobs were plentiful, but you still had to know someone to get a decent one.

At the ferry building, they were greeted with hugs and kisses by Pietro and Angelo. Since Pietro didn't own a car, he had borrowed Toe-to-Toe's car to pick up his family. The rain did not dampen their joyous reunion.

Pete was aghast at his first glimpses of The City. Driving through Chinatown, they saw chickens running wild in the streets, darting in all directions, dodging cars and people to get out of the rain. Folks with umbrellas were jumping puddles and trying to reach their destinations without getting soaked. Store windows proudly displayed dead chickens, ducks, and rabbits hanging upside down. Merchants were scrambling to pull their fresh fruit, vegetables, and clothing inside, out of the rain. The air smelled of sewer, gasoline, dead animals, rain, and Chinese spices. Pete looked in vain for a palm tree.

An electric trolley rolled by, and Pete wondered how it worked without gasoline. He wondered how the cable cars worked as well, as he watched people jumping on and off with such ease. He would soon learn all about how cable cars worked and become expert at jumping on and off without paying.

Twenty-two Cadell Place—what an enchanting sounding address! Aunt Mary's postcard with images of palm trees, green grass, and beaches with suntanned girls were pinned in Pete's mind. Then they arrived at their new home.

Cadell Place is an alley located off Union Street between Grant and Stockton Streets. An asphalt alley sandwiched between two cold-looking apartment flats; there was no grass, no palm tree, not even a flowerpot. Although extremely disappointed by his first impressions of San Francisco, Pete was very happy to see his father and brother again, and was excited about their new life in the big city.

The flat they shared was very small for two families, so the adults got the beds and the kids slept on the floor. Pete spent a lot of time outside exploring the neighborhood and many hours just sitting on the marble front steps. A restaurant called the Paper Doll was on the corner, and he soon discovered that the male cooks were doing something he had never seen. They were kissing and making out in the back kitchen, across from the steps. This was a big shock to Pete, as he had never heard of such a thing, let alone actually witness two men passionately kissing.

Across the alley from the Paper Doll on the other corner of Cadell and Union was the Marche Club occupying the second floor of the building. Pietro's hometown of Sassoferrato, Italy, is located in the region known as Marche, a beautiful farming area almost entirely overlooked by the world's tourists. Its people are called Marchigianos.

Since the immigrants who settled in San Francisco felt a connection to others who had come from their European homelands, Pietro quickly became an active member of the social club from his birthplace. It was where they met to participate in traditional Italian activities, gossip, play friendly card games, drink, and dance. There was plenty of food, as the Marche region was renowned for cuisine featuring wild game with a sauce made with rosemary, vinegar, and garlic to mask the "wild" of the meat. Chicken cacciatore was very popular, and most meals were served with creamy polenta topped with Parmesan cheese and a big hunk of sourdough bread. Jugs of house or homemade Dago Red wine completed each meal.

Members of the Marche Club were expected to take turns looking after their club. When Pete was twelve or thirteen, Pietro ask him to come to the Marche Club to help clean it. Pete had to sweep and mop the floors and wipe down the bar and tables, but the job he hated most was cleaning out the spittoons. They were stinky, disgusting, and slimy, and he begged to not do it. Pietro was a man of few words, but when he looked at Pete with "that look," Pete did what he said.

Pietro worked at Fiberboard Company during his first year in San Francisco, and his wife, Elena, quickly got a job at Zellerbach Paper Company. They began the search for a home of their own, and found a suitable flat for rent at 370 Union Street, a second-level three-bedroom apartment on Telegraph Hill at the base of Coit Tower. The first level of the building had no backyard, just a cement wall. The Mattioli backyard was about 20 by 15 feet, and was tiered up the hill. The family thought that if Coit Tower ever fell down during an earthquake, it would fall right on top of their flat.

Pete was enrolled in Garfield Elementary School, a public school located on Filbert Street. He remembers finding some rocks on the school grounds that had golden sparkles in them. Scooping them up, he ran back to his home screaming that he had found gold. His father took one look and delivered the bad news that Pete had discovered fool's gold. Adding to the disappointment, Pete had scraped up his hands digging out the golden rocks.

The kids at Garfield called Pete "The Okie" since he was from Pennsylvania and not very streetwise. They also took advantage of his small stature and relished fighting with him when he walked to and from school. He fought back and landed his share of punches, resulting in one angry mom banging on Pete's front door. Elena came to the door and told her to get the hell out of there, as her son was beat up too.

There were a few Hawaiian families who had settled into the neighborhood, and Pete befriended them quickly, deciding that he'd rather have them on his side than have to fight them all. These boys were huge, with names like Bobbo, Junior, Swaybee, Sketch, and Buddha. After he became friends with the Hawaiians, Pete seldom had to fight his way to school.

Pete's next school was Francisco Junior High on Powell between Chestnut and Francisco Streets. He certainly got a wider view of his world at Francisco, as he was one of four Caucasian kids enrolled in his homeroom class. Ninety percent of the students were Chinese. He quickly found new friends, with Al Young becoming his best friend. Pete admired Al because he earned straight A's without ever taking a book home.

Pete played soccer at Francisco Jr. High, and his team won a championship title. All players were awarded with a chenille block with a capital F to attach to their sweaters. Pete had the block for a couple of months until he earned enough money to buy a sweater.

Belonging to a club was very important to the lives of the young boys of North Beach. At Francisco Junior High, Pete and his friends formed a club called The Top Hats. They had no money for real club jackets so they stenciled the backs of their Levi jackets with a top hat and cane. They dyed their shoes with Cordovan shoe polish and then burned it into the leather with matches. The shoes shined like mirrors, and a regular spit shine kept them that way.

Pete's father, Pietro, loved to eat squabs or fledgling pigeons. He often sent Pete down to the Embarcadero piers to gather squabs from pigeon nests in the rafters. Pete became fond of pigeons, and wanted to raise them on his own. A couple of his friends were raising pigeons on their roofs, so Pete asked his Uncle Johnny to help him build a coop. Johnny had been in the U.S. Army Pigeon Signal Corps and had trained homing pigeons for reconnaissance and to fly messages back and forth.

Before long Pete had acquired and was tending to all kinds of pigeons, "homers" and "kings" in all colors. He'd release them at night to fly free. They had nests, eggs, and babies in the coop, so they would always come back home. Sometimes though, Pete's pigeons would fly over to his neighbor's coops and their pigeons would come into his. After Pete opened the door to release the pigeons, he would have to sit and wait for them to come home to close the coop door.

He decided to end this mix-up and waiting, so he cut out a hole in the middle of the coop door and attached a wooden perch to the bottom of the hole, big enough for the pigeons to land on when they returned to the coop. He cut sections of regular coat hangers and hung them from nails attached to the inside of the coop, making sure they hung down below where the perch opening was. The wires would not allow a bird to push out, but they could push the wires in from the outside to come home. After he taught the birds to push the wires in, he didn't need to worry about when the birds returned, as they would enter the coop on their own. He was very proud of his clever invention.

The city was getting complaints from neighbors about pigeon droppings on their clothes. No one had clothes dryers during that time, and most people hung their clothes on lines strung between buildings. The birds would shit on the clothes, so the City made the pigeon owners get rid of their birds. Pete was sad having to release his birds for the last time and disassemble the coop.

Most young boys in the area joined Telegraph Hill Boys and Girls Club, where Pete spent hours hanging out, playing pedro and gin rummy, and learning to box. They had regular boxing matches with the Salesian Boys and Girls Club. Both clubs had been formed to channel the unbridled energies of these young boys and curtail delinquency. There was a lot to do at the club, and Pete was a regular.

Angelo, Pete's brother, was of draft age and the Second World War was in full swing. He was working at National Biscuit Company, but he expected his call to duty at any time. Angelo was extremely excited about fighting the war for his country. Since he was working, he asked Pete to stay home from school so that he wouldn't miss the mailman when he arrived with his draft papers.

When the papers were at last delivered, Pete ran down to National Biscuit to give them to Angelo. A girl named Lillian Arentson, who also worked at National Biscuit, was in love with Angelo. She watched the exchange, and her heart sank. Angelo was dismayed when he was sent to fight in Italy. He hated the thought that he might be shooting at a cousin or some other relative.

Angelo was wounded and released from duty after earning several medals, including the Purple Heart. Lillian waited for Angelo, and they were married after he came home from the war.

The playgrounds for the boys were the streets and alleys of North Beach and Telegraph Hill. There were steps on the hill, but the kids thought it much more fun to crawl all over the rocky steep terrain like little spiders, exploring every nook and crevice. They knew every inch, every rock, and who lived in all the homes that hung like Christmas ornaments on the sides of the hill.

After slithering down the craggy eastside cliffs, they would land in the warehouse district, where they roamed around looking for something to do. This area was full of huge warehouses, trucks, and trains. Produce was brought in from the valley by rail and truck and stored in refrigerated warehouses. It was the center of distribution for all kinds of products for domestic use and the war effort. It was also the Army's main distribution center for war supplies. The boxcars were sealed, and it was a federal offense to cut the wire on the seal. But the seals were often broken and the boxcars pilfered. Pete and his friends would steal watermelons, throw a few into an old crate, and drag the booty up Kearny Street for a feast.

The boys used to chase the Army flatbed trucks used to transport G.I. jackets and boots. The heavy trucks with solid rubber tires couldn't go very fast through the city streets, so they were vulnerable. One boy would jump on the truck and throw boots and coats out for the other boys to catch and bundle. They would sell them on street corners in the City.

"We were poor," Pete later said. "We took advantage of whatever we could get. We didn't hurt nobody. We didn't shoot anybody. If I got caught for all the things I did as a teen, though, I'd still be in San Quentin."

Pietro and Elena took in boarders from time to time to help pay the rent. Peppe was one of the men who lived at the Mattioli flat. His work took him all over the world, including Saudi Arabia. He would work on a project for a year or two and come home with a big stack of money. Pietro used to make Pete go with Peppe to Falchi's, a restaurant across the street from the Fior De Italia, to watch over him, as he knew that he would become so inebriated he may not find his way home. Pete would sit and wait in the corner of the entrance while Peppe got plastered. His job was to help him climb up the hill to their flat. Peppe always made sure Pete had lots of candy, comic books, and soda pop. He gave him money, too.

"He took my room, and I slept on the floor or couch," Pete recalls. "Uncle Gino and Cousin Rudy took my room too when they came home from the war. Everybody had priority but me at my house. Whenever we had people staying with us, they'd kick me out. I was just a kid, anyways, so I could sleep anywhere."

Pete did whatever he could to make a little money. Thousands of G.I.s were passing through San Francisco and processed at the USO in the Pepsi Cola Center on Market Street. It seemed like they all wanted mirror-shiny shoes. Pete and his father made a shoeshine box out of an old apple crate. Pete would walk to Market Street carrying his crate full of rags and shoe polish through the tunnel on Stockton Street. There was an alcove at the entrance of the USO where all the shoeshine kids hung out. While shining their shoes, Pete would engage the soldier in conversation. "I'll bet I can tell you how many kids your father had," he would say.

"I'll bet you can't. You don't even know me," was the soldier's usual answer.

"None," after agreeing to the bet, Pete would say with a big grin. "Your mother had them all." When the squirming G.I. would say that wasn't fair, the other guys would yell out, "Pay the kid." Pete thought he was pretty damned smart, getting away with that one. The kids charged ten cents a shine but sometimes Pete made more money with his trick questions than by shining shoes.

Pete went down to Market Street on VJ (Victory over Japan) Day. He climbed up on a street lamp for a better view, then onto a statue by the Pepsi Cola Center to watch the celebrations. People were breaking the display windows of businesses, and looting. The Emporium department store was being renovated, and there was huge scaffolding on the side of the building. People had climbed up onto the scaffolding and were swinging like monkeys. Thousands of people lined the street. The mob was tipping over cars, stealing fur coats and jewelry from stores; things were out of control. Pete watched as one woman took her coat off and was swinging it. Some men in the crowd stripped her naked and mauled her. They pinched and groped her until the police finally arrived.

He and his friends often hitchhiked out to Playland at the Beach and Sutro Baths at Land's End on the westernmost end of San Francisco. If they were lucky, they could grab the back of a streetcar and hang on for a free ride to Ocean Beach.

Pete's mother, Elena, was very religious and attended mass at Saints Peter and Paul, a Catholic church on Filbert Street, across the street from Washington Square. His father refused to go into a church, any church, often taking his wife to Mass and waiting for her outside the church or drinking a beer at a local bar. Elena's mother, Lucia, lived with them, but suffered from dementia and would often wander around the neighborhood, forgetting the way home. They usually found her in prayer at Saints Peter and Paul.

One day Pete decided to hide his grandmother's false teeth. He grabbed them off the counter and ran outside the flat and down the street. He can still visualize his grandmother hanging out the window, pumping her fists and yelling, "Hey, you little *bastardo*! Come back with my teeth!"

Family gatherings were frequent, with picnics in the Washington Square Park or weekend visits with family. Whenever someone visited the Mattioli household, Pietro would instruct Pete to polish all the men's shoes with supplies from his new shoeshine box.

Pete enrolled in Galileo High School in the fall of 1947. He was excited to meet new friends and become part of the iconic institution with the fierce lion mascot. One of his idols, Joe DiMaggio, had attended Galileo, even though he never graduated, dropping out in 1930. Almost as famous at the time was All-Star Gino Cimoli, who had graduated in 1947 and played for the Brooklyn Dodgers, St. Louis Cardinals, and Pittsburg Pirates.

Pete loved to swim and quickly joined the swim team. He took classes in auto shop and cabinet making. He enjoyed those classes, but reading, writing and arithmetic, well, not so much.

Pete met the Lombardi brothers, John and Mario, at Galileo High, where they became fast friends. They had a vivacious and fun younger sister named Carmella. The Lombardi brothers had formed a club called the Bruins. They sported a blue athletic jacket with white sleeves. Embroidered on the left chest of the jacket was a large bear with the club name, "Bruins," underneath. The member's name was written in cursive

North Beach gang hanging out at Mike's soda fountain on Chestnut Street. (Pete is standing at back.)

above the bear. The rest of the club "uniform" consisted of a white T-shirt, low-slung cuffed pants, white socks, and black-laced shoes. Pete joined the Bruins and felt like he belonged.

The Bruins were the cool popular guys, not necessarily rich, but the athletic and handsome boys of Galileo High. Some of the members besides John and Mario Lombardi were Eddie Belasco, Richard Isless, Bob Gilardi, Eddie Garcia, brothers Gig and Chud Duncan, Nasius Marinelli, Jim Faber, and twins Allen and Arlen Bragg. They hung out at now famous spots like Ott's Drive-in, located at Bay and Columbus Avenues, and several soda fountains, including the Cream Cup across the street from the Telegraph Hill Boys Club.

Another classmate was Frankie Alioto, whose father, Nunzio, owned a crab stand at Fisherman's Wharf. During Pete's first year of high school, he and John Lombardi worked cracking crab at the stand. Since Frankie was always late for work, Nunzio bought him a car, with an order for him to get to work on time. Frankie was one of the good guys, and the only one of the young men who had a car, so everyone wanted to be friends with him. Sometimes they piled seven or eight kids into that car to cruise around the City. Then John Lombardi got a car, and *he* quickly became the big man around town.

Eddie Belasco dated a beautiful young lady named Dolores Rose at Galileo, and Pete had secretly fallen in love with her. When she broke up with Eddie, Pete made his move and dated her for a year or so. She lived a couple of miles from Pete, and he would walk the distance to see her. She was from a very poor family who treated her badly. She had very few clothes to wear, but she was creative in sewing her brother's clothing into fashionable items that were feminine enough for a lady to wear. Dolores was very pretty and wanted to be an actress. Pete always thought she was "his girl," but soon found out that she was "everybody's girl," dating several guys at the same time. She was Pete's first big crush and first broken heart. (Dolores later moved to Los Angeles to pursue an acting career, which never materialized. Depressed by her failure to become a movie star, she ended her life by slitting her wrists and driving her car into the Hollywood Bowl. Her death has haunted Pete his entire life.)

The boys of North Beach loved to play and chase girls at the Russian River area during the 1950s. Sometimes one of them would drive up, but many times they simply hitchhiked up the Redwood Highway until they arrived in Rio Nido or Guerneville. Often it took a full day to get there. In order to eat, they would do odd jobs for the different businesses. A half-day's work often resulted in a hamburger, fries, and a shake, possibly even a ticket to one of the dances. Most of the cabins were owned by wealthy city dwellers who only spent summers at the river. Pete and his friends were always on the lookout for one of the daughters to play with and provide them with food and booze.

Never one for good study habits or attendance at Galileo High, Pete quit school when he was sixteen. Later realizing that he needed a high school degree, he enrolled in Continuation School and eventually earned his GED diploma from Chase High School.

Pete had several jobs during his teen years, including delivering ravioli for Amerigo Del Prete, who owned Panama Ravioli Factory on Grant

Pete (front row, 2nd from right) and his high school buddies.

Avenue. His son, Gino, was one of Pete's high school friends. Amerigo
had named his company after the then newly completed Panama Canal,
which he considered one of the wonders of the world, creating great
commerce throughout the globe as well. He figured the name would also
bring success to his business. Pete saw firsthand what made up the filling
for the ravioli, which was comprised of ground beef and other beef parts,
including brains and organs. Nevertheless, the raviolis were delicious
and in high demand. Pete delivered them to small markets and restaurants throughout the City.

Pete's father worked at O'Brien, Sportono, Compano, and Mitchell on
Clay Street, a poultry processing business. It was a disgusting job, but
paid well. His job was to feed and care for the chickens until slaughter,
gathering eggs and keeping their pens clean. The trays of poop needed
to be emptied and rinsed often.

The chickens were hung by their feet and attached to a conveyer belt.
The man responsible for slitting their throats was never without his
blood-spattered cigar, ever burning to diminish the stench. After the
chickens were killed, they traveled into a machine spraying boiling hot

water and tossing them to remove the feathers. The chickens were then sent into a room where women worked to remove the remaining feathers. When Pete was sixteen and attending Continuation School, he got a job wrapping the heads of the chickens. He was also responsible for grading the chickens, A, B, C, "water belly," etc., before they were sent to market.

At times, the poultry plant also processed rabbits, imported from Australia, which had been frozen and arrived on rail cars. Pete's job was to skin them. Since they were frozen solid, it was very difficult to pull the skin off, and his hands became numb with cold. The bones of the rabbit cut into his flesh, but he didn't feel the pain until afterward when his hands warmed up.

Brother Angelo worked at Sunset Poultry on Irving at 41st Street. Pete drove the delivery truck and sold chickens over the counter. It was here he learned the skills of "cheating the customer just a bit" when he was told to cut a small piece of the liver from each chicken sold for "the house." That little bit of liver would later be sold, but without any cost to the owner of the business. He noticed another trick of the trade when he saw that the boss had strategically placed a fan above the meat scale. That fan produced just enough downward airflow to tip the scales in favor of the business owner.

Pete then worked at a cheese factory on Clay Street, dipping soft Parmesan cheese in paraffin and, after it hardened, oiling the paraffin. He hated this job as his 4-foot-3-inch boss was constantly sneaking around the cheese room, peering through the rows of cheese to be sure Pete was working. He quit after two weeks.

Aunt Mary and Uncle Toe-to-Toe had moved out to the Sunset District, where new homes were being built in what was known as the Dunes. Sand dunes. Pietro took his family to visit often, sometimes toting rifles to shoot jackrabbits. Pete loved to visit his uncle and aunt, and remembers once trying to sneak a peek under Aunt Mary's skirt as she climbed a ladder to change a light bulb.

Uncle Toe-to-Toe worked digging ditches for Scott Company, one of the firms contracted to build the infrastructure for the Sunset homes. Pete's family thought that the families of the Sunset were rich, living in new homes with good heating, nice bathrooms, and carpeted living rooms. One day, Pete was working alongside his Uncle Toe-to-Toe, shoveling sand out of a pit just a little faster than the sand was falling back in. Suddenly, Toe-to-Toe was buried up to his neck as the sand caved in on him. Everyone on the job grabbed their shovels and began frantically digging him out. He was almost buried alive, but was saved by his fellow workers.

There actually was a beach in North Beach, and Pete found it eventually—a tiny sliver of sand and pebbles in front of a bathhouse built to look like a ship. Aquatic Park had been constructed during the Great Depression by orders from President Franklin Roosevelt, who believed that people needed a place to gather and enjoy their families and the outdoors. After Pete discovered it, he swam there often with his buddies and although they might see a turd float by once in a while, they didn't make a fuss about it. Swimming was better than not swimming and while there were no palm trees, there were plenty of pretty girls to meet.

3

In the Navy

Pete joined the U.S. Navy in January of 1951. The Korean War was raging. Many of his high school buddies had already joined or been drafted, so he figured he'd better join. Mario Lombardi and Islas Garcia joined the Marines. Nacius Marinelli joined the Army. Jim Faber, Frank Alioto, and Ed Garcia joined the Navy. Pete wanted to choose his branch of service. He loved the water and figured his chances of coming home alive during wartime were best in the Navy, so he signed up. All his San Francisco friends threw a big drunken going-away party for him when he left for boot camp.

Like most sailors, he completed his Naval training in San Diego, California. It was at boot camp where Pete experienced his first real encounter with racism. While he was washing his clothes, he noticed some sailors from Texas picking on a black sailor for no apparent reason. He told them, "Leave the kid alone. He's not bothering you." For a little guy, Pete wasn't afraid to express his mind to some of the bullies in the Navy. The black sailor came over to Pete, thanked him, and tried to stay close to him after that.

In his everyday encounters with other sailors, he heard and saw many accounts of racism. One of the white sailors told Pete that where he was from, they made the niggers walk in the gutter when passing a white man on a sidewalk. Pete could hardly believe it. Things were different in California. African Americans drank from the same water fountains and ate at the same restaurants as whites. Pete was disgusted at hearing these stories and hated the cruelty contained in them.

He was stunned when he learned his first assignment was at Hunter's Point Naval Shipyard back in San Francisco. Back home! He would have to wait to go see the world. When he returned to San Francisco from boot camp, he called his buddies to let them know he was back. They met up at Pucci's Bar on Lombard Street and drank to their reunion.

Pete's Navy buddies at Hunter's Point were receiving transfer notices to exotic places like Hawaii and Japan. "Everybody's getting transferred but me," Pete complained. He turned in chit after chit requesting a transfer; he wanted to sail on a ship. He requested assignment on a battlewagon, and was refused. He wanted to go on a cruiser, but was again turned down.

Bobby Mezzanatto, a friend of Pete's when they were teenagers, was also stationed at Hunter's Point, although he was in the Marines. He and Pete were always in trouble with their superiors for not wearing their hats and often sneaking in late after a night of partying. Bobby's commanding officer threatened to take his stripes if he checked in late one more time.

Of course, it happened again.

So Bobby came up with a plan. He decided to fake mental illness. He began his act of talking to himself and making crazy, off-the-wall remarks. It wasn't long before he was placed in the psychiatric ward at Oak Knoll Hospital in Oakland. Pete visited him often, but one occasion was special. When Pete met up with Bobby at the hospital, he saw that Bobby had lined up a few chairs and was pushing them up and down the hall, calling out "choo, choo." They could hardly contain their laughter as they successfully kept Bobby's secret between them. There wasn't a thing wrong with Bobby's mental capabilities, and he was eventually discharged with all his stripes intact.

Pete recalls, "So I was just living my normal life in the City, going down on Lombard Street to Pucci's and getting drunk. One night when I returned to Hunter's Point, I had a transfer notice. Wow, I'm getting transferred! I was so excited I got drunk for a whole week. I didn't know or care where I was going to, but it was a transfer."

Then Pete got the papers. It was to Alameda Naval Air Station, located on the east shore of San Francisco Bay! His buddies asked him if he knew someone who was pulling strings to keep him in the Bay Area. Why did *he* get to stay in San Francisco? Pete didn't know anyone and wanted to transfer out of the Bay Area, but he didn't get to choose where he was sent.

His Navy uniform was blue with white stripes, but now he was issued new green stripes for his uniform, signaling that he was now Naval Air. Pete had never seen an airplane up close, only in the sky. He walked into a hangar and was awestruck by the size of the Navy jets, Grumman F9F Panthers, parked inside for repair. The Panther was the first military jet manufactured by Grumman and was also the first jet used by the Blue Angels fight team. The Navy and Marine Corp used it extensively during the Korean War. Pete wondered what he was supposed to do with them.

He was sent to Moffett Field for two weeks training in airframe and the dual hydraulics systems of the Panther. He learned how to patch up the holes and ripped-up sheet metal in the airframe after they had been damaged in battles. He was taught how to repair the complicated hydraulic systems. He returned to Alameda to begin his new assignments.

Pete's commander had set up some strict rules for behavior at Alameda. If one of the sailors had a beef with another, they had to wait until the monthly picnic to settle it. The commander would set up a boxing ring where the two would box it out. The whole squadron looked forward to these fights and would gather around for the match, which would be settled right then and there.

While at Alameda, Pete was sent out to sea on the USS *Yorktown* (CV-10) aircraft carrier for a daylong shakedown cruise, a nautical term used when a ship is taken to sea to test its performance and operational systems. It is usually done when a ship is newly launched or after a ship has received a major overhaul. This was very exciting for Pete, his first trip at sea. The next week, he was sent out for another shakedown cruise, this time on the USS *Boxer* (CV-21). The *Boxer* was already a well-respected and famous aircraft carrier within Navy ranks, as it had survived several battles of Korean War.

Pete continued to work in Alameda. He bought an old Pontiac car, and speedily crashed it in the Alameda Tunnel. Cleaning crews were hosing down the roadbed inside tunnel as he entered. The asphalt was slick, and Pete hit another car head-on. Both drivers were drunk and ended up in the hospital. Both cars were totaled, but neither driver sustained serious injuries. At the court hearing, Pete's defending officer didn't show up, so Pete defended himself. He cited the slick road, and the case was dismissed.

Pete reported for duty the next day and was handed a transfer notice. "Oh, shit. Guam?" Pete questioned.

"You've got it," stated his commander. "You wanted a transfer out of the Bay Area so here you are."

"Where's Guam?" Pete replied.

"Way the hell out in the Pacific Ocean, past Hawaii," was the reply.

This time Pete had a really big going-away party. He knew that once he was transferred to Guam, he would be there at least a year. He got drunk with his buddies, said his goodbyes, and boarded a ship headed for Guam. He was very excited. It was July of 1953.

The *USNS Barrett* (T-AP-196) was a troop transport ship, launched in 1950 and acquired by the Navy in 1952. She already had served three tours in the Korean War when Pete climbed aboard. They sailed under the Golden Gate Bridge, all the sailors full of anticipation and adventure. Their first stop was a short one in Honolulu, where they took on supplies.

On July 13, 1953, somewhere west of Wake Island, the *Barrett* received a radio message that a plane had gone down in the Pacific. It was immediately dispatched to the crash scene to rescue any survivors. The airplane was a Transocean Airlines "Royal Hawaiian" Flight #512, destined for Honolulu. The flight had originated in Guam and had 58 passengers aboard. The *Barrett* arrived about eight hours after the plane crashed, and found the *USS Tomahawk* also on the scene.

There was extensive debris floating in the water, and many bodies. They could see four deflated and one inflated raft, but no survivors. Dozens of sharks had arrived and were in process of devouring the victims. Both ships launched lifeboats with crews. The sailors began plucking charred and mutilated bodies and body parts from the water. When they realized that there were no survivors, they began to worry about the safety of the lifeboat crews due to the shark frenzy going on. The *Barrett* recovery effort was called off after recovering only fourteen bodies. The *USS Tomahawk* recovered three bodies and transferred them to the *Barrett*.

The bodies were taken to the refrigeration units of the *Barrett* and placed on the floor, alongside the eggs, bacon, and milk. Knowing this, the sailors had a hard time choking down their chow that evening and their breakfast the next morning.

A few days later the sailors got their first glimpse of Guam, a tiny little speck of an island on the horizon. The sight of its diminutive size brought anguish to many who had trouble contemplating living a year of their lives there.

Guam is the largest of the Mariana Islands, but is still very small, only 209 square miles. It was captured by the Japanese on December 8,1941, hours after the attack on Pearl Harbor, recaptured by the U.S. on July 21, 1944 (which is now celebrated by Guamanians as Liberation Day), and continues to be a territory of the United States.

They arrived in Guam to a temperature of 95 degrees and 95 percent humidity. Pete had never felt such heat. All sailors were placed in hand-to-hand combat and martial arts training.

Pete was assigned a Quonset hut and told to paint it. He was working alongside another sailor and found out that his last name was actually "Sailor." Pete thought that was hilarious, and they became fast friends. While painting the Quonset hut they began talking about swimming, and Pete told him he used to swim in San Francisco Bay and a place called Sutro Baths out by Ocean Beach. Sailor mentioned that they were looking for a lifeguard for Tumon Beach, Guam's largest but most neglected beach.

"Do you know the lieutenant?" Pete asked.

"Yeah," Sailor replied. "I'll talk to him."

Pete was called into the lieutenant's office the next day.

"I understand you're a lifeguard," the lieutenant said.

"Yes, sir," Pete replied, even though he had never been a real lifeguard.

Pete (far right) and other Navy lifeguards at Tumon Beach.

"Do you have a Red Cross card?" he asked.

"No, sir. I didn't think of bringing it to Guam," Pete replied.

"Will you take the test again?" the lieutenant inquired.

"Yes, sir," Pete affirmed.

Pete took the test and became a lifeguard at Tumon Bay, on a beach controlled by the United States Air Force. The head of the Air Force Police was a sergeant from Louisiana named John Quincy Hyde, whom Pete had befriended. Another guy, a Native American Air Force sergeant, had been in charge of the beach, but was transferred back to the States, and the Air Force had given his job to Hyde. He didn't want the job.

Hyde asked Pete, "Do you want to be in charge of this beach?"

"Sure, why not?" was Pete's answer. "If you'll back me up."

Within two months he had been promoted to head lifeguard. Pete couldn't believe his luck. His buddies were over in Korea getting shot up or killed and here he was, the head lifeguard of Tumon Beach. Tough duty.

As head lifeguard, he was given his own little shack, complete with a small bunk and lockers. He had to wear his Navy whites and report for special occasions, but other than that, he lived in his swimsuit and stayed at the beach. He showered in the clubhouse. Pete's chief petty officer was irritated by the freedom Pete enjoyed.

Tumon Beach was over 1,000 yards long, and was segregated. Not by race, but by rank. The best part was reserved for officers, then noncommissioned officers, the enlisted, and lastly, the natives. It was all sectioned and roped off. People knew where they did and didn't belong.

Pete got to work cleaning up the beach. He had visions of Waikiki Beach, which he had seen on his way to Guam. He was disgusted by what he had seen on Tumon Beach. Trash, sea slugs, seaweed, and driftwood were everywhere. The creepy dark brown sea slugs lay in the shallow water just off the beach. They were as big as cucumbers, and if you stepped on one, it would squirt a gluey white substance that stuck to your feet. There were a few old beat-up garbage cans resting on the sand.

One day he walked into the back room of Hyde's shack and saw dozens of umbrellas neatly stacked in the corner. He opened a couple, and found they were ripped and full of holes. Next to them were about ten eleven-foot-long surfboards that had rough broken edges and needed caulking and sanding.

He told the lifeguards, "No more ping-pong, guys. See all these umbrellas? They're torn. Get them out of this shack and fix them. Sew up the holes. Look at these surfboards. I'm assigning a board to each one of you. I want you to caulk it, sand it, and varnish it. It had better look good, and I want it that way all the time. That's your job."

When they finished repairing the umbrellas, they loaded them onto a weapons carrier truck and drove the beach, dropping them about every ten yards or so, sticking them in the sand and opening them up. The beach was beginning to take shape.

Pete had heard of an abandoned airstrip. He decided to look around to see if there was anything they could use at the beach. He found several 55-gallon drums. They dumped the sand out, painted them, and placed them along the beach as garbage cans. Then he found some buoys and roped off a safe swimming area in the water. He found an 8-by-10 sheet of plywood. He hammered dozens of nails into it, then placed another plywood sheet on top and nailed them together. Then he attached two 12-foot cables, which he connected to a weapons carrier. That made for a great little drag to clean and flatten the sand. When he finished, Tumon Beach was beautiful. It looked almost as good as Waikiki.

"They thought I was nuts," recalls Pete.

Then he started getting the calls. Some of the admirals and captains had seen the umbrellas and requested them for their backyards up by the U.S. Naval Base or Anderson Air Force Base. Pete transported around twenty umbrellas up to the officer housing units.

The beach became very popular, especially with the women, as it was now clean and beautiful. There were some women in the services stationed at Guam, but most women there were military wives or civilians. It was a hotbed for sex, cheating spouses, and lonely men and women. Pete had a months-long affair with a waitress named LaVonne, a beautiful blonde twice his age.

While in Guam, Pete became especially close to another lifeguard, an African-American sailor named Jim Partee. Jim was from Louisiana and had experienced racism at its worst. He worked out and did whatever he could to build his body into a beautiful sculpture of muscle. Jim decided he would learn how to box, and soon became the light heavyweight champion of Guam Island. Even though he could have knocked anyone on their ass, Jim showed constraint in all he did.

Partee was extremely polite to everyone. He was impressively fit and kept in shape by running down to the beach from the Naval Base in Agana instead of hitching a ride on the weapons carrier with the other sailors. Jim usually left early in order to be there when the others arrived. He slept above Pete in the barracks, and they became good friends. Pete wanted Partee on his side if there was ever a dispute.

Drinking beer was the biggest pastime for the sailors stationed at Guam; there were barrels full of Budweiser at every gathering. They caught fish, grilled them on beach-wood bonfires, and washed them down with beer, beer, and more beer. If a sailor got too drunk, they dragged him into the clubhouse and threw him in the shower for a quick sober-up.

The squadron priest, Father Agnew, was often at the beach, and joined the beer drinking parties. If Pete was ever late getting back to the barracks, Father Agnew would call and tell the on-duty officer that Pete was with him. No more questions were asked.

In Guam there were all kinds of bugs that Pete had never seen before. Flying and crawling bugs. One night while Pete was asleep in his shack on the beach, a moth flew into his ear. It buried itself deep in his ear canal and sounded like a B-29 buzzing in there until it finally died a few hours later. He had to wait till morning to go to the infirmary, where they flushed it out.

Typhoons were a constant threat at Guam and several occurred while Pete was stationed there. He received a commendation for bravery for rescuing a sailor in an incident that occurred a couple of days after one had hit Guam. Pete, dressed in his Navy whites after being treated at the base hospital for the flu, received word that someone was drowning out in the huge waves still coming ashore from the typhoon.

His first reaction was, "What the hell is anyone doing swimming out there in those rough seas? Probably a damned officer."

He stripped off his whites and put his bathing suit on. Then he threw two surfboards on a weapons carrier and drove to another beach for a better view. He saw the man struggling out in the water. Pete was with another lifeguard who was in the Air Force and barely knew how to swim.

They threw their boards into the dangerous waves and began to paddle. Pete watched the Air Force lifeguard turn back. Then he saw his friend Hyde paddling out, but he also turned back.

Pete battled through twenty-foot waves and finally made it out to the drowning officer. He saw that the Marines had dropped a raft from a plane, which the officer had pulled himself into. Pete paddled up beside the raft and saw that the officer's body was bloodied up from being thrown against the reef.

"Any paddles in there?" Pete yelled.

"No," was the reply.

Pete told him to help pull his board up onto the raft, and he would push him ashore. They got the long board onto the raft and Pete began to swim and push, push and swim, until he was so exhausted, he clung to the raft while he caught his breath and rested. Then he saw the words "Oars," printed on the inside of the raft.

"You stupid son of a bitch!" Pete screamed at the guy. "What the hell does that say?"

Pete pulled himself into the raft and unlatched the oars. They both paddled until the Marines sent out a cruiser, threw them a line, and towed them to shore.

Pete received a commendation letter at a small ceremony, and the officer gave him $25 in cash. He bought a few cases of Budweiser with the money and shared them with the guys on the beach.

Pete served eighteen months on Guam and has often said that he had the "dumbest career in the Navy." He wanted to do something more important. But given the choice, being lifeguard with all its perks vs. fighting in Korea? Well, he thought, someone had to do it, but Pete couldn't believe he was the one.

He received an honorable discharge in 1954.

4

The Country Boy
and the City Boy

The Japanese government surrendered after the second nuclear bomb was dropped on Nagasaki in August of 1945, bringing an end to the conflict in the Pacific. People who lived on the West Coast were greatly relieved, as they had been living with the ever-present threat of a Japanese attack on one of the major cities. Their fears generated a profound sense that, even after the war ended, they were still vulnerable to an attack of some kind. Many decided to move to inland locations they perceived as safer for their families. The city of Fresno, located about half way between Los Angeles and San Francisco, grew substantially due to people migrating from the major coastal cities. Pete's father, Pietro, shared this fear and decided it was time to relocate. He found fifty acres of vineyard land on which an old house sat in Selma, a tiny town south of Fresno in the fertile heart of Central California's agricultural region, and proceeded to purchase it.

Pietro's friends at the Marche Club in San Francisco argued with each other to decide who would lend Pietro the money to buy the land in the Central Valley. They all wanted to help him out. He borrowed the money from a man named Scarcucci, who owned a cement company. After he began his vineyard operation, he drove back to San Francisco each month to make his loan payment to Scarcucci.

After Pete was discharged from the Navy, he moved to Selma to help his father with the vineyard. He had sent money home each month from his Navy paycheck and his father had saved it for him. He gave it back to Pete when he joined him in Selma. Pete bought a used Ford convertible with the money and tried to get used to his new environment.

They grew mostly Thompson seedless, muscat, and table grapes. When Pietro wasn't happy with the price offered for his grapes, he would dry them, turning them into raisins, and give them to the Sun-Maid co-op to sell. Pete's brother, Angelo, also moved to Selma with his wife, Lillian; daughter, Cheryl; and son, Kenny. Angelo obtained a Cal Vet loan and became a partner with his dad in the vineyard. They worked as a family tending the vines, pruning and picking grapes, and flipping raisin trays. Pietro always grew enough red wine grapes to sell—and to keep a big jug of wine on the dinner table.

It was hard, tedious work in extremely hot weather, but Pietro loved it. Next to the house was a large cement water storage tank used for irrigation, but big enough and deep enough to use as a swimming pool. Tire inner tubes served as floats, and everyone plunged in after a hot day in the fields.

Pietro's birthplace, Sassoferrato, is in the Marche region of Italy, which is not as famous as the Chianti region but it produces excellent wine, especially white Verdicchio and garnet-colored Sangiovese. Pietro wanted to follow in his father's footsteps, and had a lifetime dream of owning his own vineyard and producing wine. He was never happier than the years in Selma, farming and enjoying his family.

Toe-to-Toe, Pietro's brother-in-law, moved to Selma as well, and became a third partner in the vineyard business. They seldom saw eye-to-eye about the everyday details of working the vineyard. Pietro meticulously cared for the land, and felt that "Toe" was always cutting corners and trying to get things done too quickly. One day Pietro found a grapevine wilting in the sun. Upon closer inspection, he found that it had been ripped from the ground by the tractor and just stuck back into the soil. Toe-to-Toe had hoped that his carelessness wouldn't be noticed, but of course, Pietro saw the withered plant, and blew his top. Constantly arguing over vineyard management, Pietro eventually bought out Toe-to-Toe, but retained the partnership with his son, Angelo.

Pete gave the family vineyard business a good go, but soon discovered that living in Selma was a planet away from the life he knew in San Francisco. He longed for the City.

While working the midnight shift at a gas station, a young lady friend began stopping by to spend a little time with Pete when business was slow. They did nothing more than play cards, but it seemed to Pete like the whole town was watching them through the large plate glass window. Pete's mother had cautioned him on several occasions, "Pete, don't ruin the family name!" Pete hated the small town where everyone gossiped and knew everything that was going on. He detested the heat, and just didn't feel like he fit in with the community. He longed for the cool gray City by the Bay that offered privacy—and held secrets. Pete told his family that he would be going back to San Francisco to live. He packed up his Ford convertible and headed back to his old neighborhood, North Beach.

Pete arrived back in San Francisco with only a few dollars in his pocket. He contacted his high school buddy Frankie Alioto and asked to borrow some money to get set up in an apartment. Frankie trusted that he would pay him back, and gladly handed over $150. Pete moved into a basement apartment on Pleasant Street in the Nob Hill area and got a job at American Can Company on Third Street that same day.

His landlady, Mrs. Newhall, lived above the tiny basement apartment across from Nob Hill Grocery. The entrance was down a small passageway, and Pete had rigged up a scary scenario for anyone opening the entry door. He had placed a tiny iguana figurine upon the mantle, with a lighted Belfast clock placed directly behind. The light in the clock projected a huge shadow of the iguana on the wall, scaring the wits out of anyone who entered and was unaware of it.

One night, two of Pete's friends—Paul Svetkoff, a bartender at the El Matador, and Roy Hunter, a Seaman's Union of the Pacific goon squad member—got into a fight and trashed Pete's apartment, punching a big hole in the wall. Pete decided he'd better move out. Sweet Mrs. Newhall never made Pete fix it up or pay for the damages.

Pete moved into a two-bedroom six-unit apartment building on Sutter and Jones Street with Artie Gonzalez, a friend who worked at the Hamm's Brewery. He soon noticed that their building was very busy with men, coming and going, going and coming. There were always "broads" running in and out.

"What the hell's going on, Artie?"

"It's a whorehouse, didn't you know that?" was Artie's reply.

Pete didn't mind that; in fact, he liked the idea. They later learned that at least one of the apartments served as a brothel, complete with whips, chains, and belts commonly used in sadomasochistic adult sex play in which certain people derive pleasure from inflicted pain.

He and Artie became friends with the madam and her sister, and soon became regular visitors at the other apartments. On one of these visits, they encountered their first cross-dresser. The man wanted be chased around the coffee table and then whipped. They obliged with a couple of cracks of a whip, which absolutely delighted him, and were rewarded with free lays from a couple of the gals. Pete became more than friends with the madam's sister, who was soon telling him she was in love with him. That made for an uncomfortable relationship and soon afterward, they moved out.

Pete's job at American Can Company was working on the boxing line, making a game out of filling the boxes before the box-making machine could make another box. In another department, employees had to stack coffee cans in railroad boxcars for shipment. The area was full of huge warehouses and rail cars; it was where most goods were shipped in and out of San Francisco.

Most of the people worked boring assembly line jobs, so they were inclined to do whatever they could get away with to break the monotony. They told jokes, played tricks on each other, and tried to make things fun. They made eyes at each other too, and when no one was looking, might even get away with a little screwing in one of the boxcars. Of course, you would be fired immediately if caught.

Pete's boss at American Can Company was a lesbian named Reba, who invited him and his new roommate, Artie Gonzalez, to several undercover parties. Pete couldn't get over the beautiful women who were kissing each other at these affairs. Pete and Artie sat around the room with huge hard-ons, but no one there was interested in them.

Homosexual activity was illegal in those days. If arrested, you could lose your job, your apartment, and go to jail. Anyone attending these parties in the '50s and early '60s knew that a police raid was very possible at any time. So, upon arriving, Pete and Artie would try to figure out where the back door or window was and how to get out in a hurry if necessary. They found themselves scampering down fire escapes or across rooftops on several occasions.

Pete quit his job at American Can Company and took a job at Hamm's Brewery, south of Market Street, where Artie worked. It was another assembly line job, in which he was charged with inspecting the beer bottles for clarity. He also took a job delivering ravioli for Panama Canal Ravioli, which was owned by his friend Gino Del Prete's father, Amerigo, and his partner, Del Pagitto. The partners were constantly discussing their "big money" investments and checking their penny stock purchases, especially Kennecott Copper Company.

After work, Pete would meet all his buddies at Pucci's House of Pisco— which was in due time to be called the Condor—on Columbus and Broadway for drinks. Mario Puccinelli was a big, burly former football player with curly hair and a big handlebar moustache, who had previously owned a bar on Lombard Street called Pucci's, where Pete and his buddies had hung out before he went into the Navy. Pucci loved women and was quite likable, but had no finesse or manners whatsoever. He would occasionally ask, "Hey, Pete, watch the place? I'll be right back."

Pete had never bartended, so he would ask the patrons what was in the drinks they ordered and mix them up. Two a.m. would arrive with no sight of Pucci, and Pete had no keys to lock up, so he would have to wait. Pucci always came stumbling back in the wee hours to lock the door.

Eventually Mario Puccinelli took Gino Del Prete as his partner at the House of Pisco. The bar was losing money, so Pucci decided to turn it over to Del Prete, and accepted a job as beverage manager at the Iron Horse on Maiden Lane.

While working at Pucci's, Pete quickly picked up the skills he would need later when he landed a bartending job at the famous

Polynesian-themed Trader Vic's Restaurant on Cosmo Place, owned by Vic Bergeron. He worked the Trader Vic's service bar nights, sunbathed and chased women at Aquatic Park during the day. His Navy buddy Bobby Mezzanatto, a Marine who had been stationed with him at Hunter's Point Naval Air Station in San Francisco, also worked there.

Sometimes they would babysit Bobby's toddler son in the service bar at Trader Vic's, and even looked after Bergeron's young son there. Occasionally, they hid Bobby in the back storage room when the police came in looking for him to collect child support for his boy.

One of the older bartenders at Trader Vic's retired, so Pete was promoted to the main dining room bar. Work was much more exciting out there, as you got to mingle with San Francisco's social elites who were regular diners at the restaurant. Plus, he made much more in tips. There was one regular who ordered his martini "extra dry, on the rocks, and stirred ten times." He never accepted the first martini served, the second, or the third. Usually he would agree that the fourth martini was "just perfect" and drink it. Pete got a kick out of this, as all he had done was pour the first martini into another glass each time, allowing the ice to melt a bit until it was "just perfect."

Trader Vic's specialized in unique, potent rum cocktails and claimed to have created the original Mai Tai drink. The drinks were practically a floorshow. The Scorpion could be served as an individual drink or mixed in a large ceramic bowl decorated with Polynesian figures; gardenias floated atop and several straws were provided for people to share. The Fog Cutter was served in a tall Chinese ceramic mug, again adorned with island figures. The Kamiana was poured into a real coconut shell with a slapped fresh mint leaf, adding to the deliciousness. The Tahitian Pearl was served in a clear-stemmed glass, with a pearl delicately placed on a floating gardenia petal, very feminine. Bergeron bought large bags of the pearls, but women thought it very special when they were served a drink adorned with one. Many ladies saved the single cultured pearl hoping to collect enough to make a pearl necklace. It would take a long time to accomplish that feat, as one drink would usually knock them out.

The menu featured exotic dishes such as rumaki (water chestnuts and chicken livers wrapped in bacon) and Chinese barbecue, introducing this style of cuisine to a new clientele. Cooking was displayed through clear glass oven doors, adding to the distinctiveness of the restaurant. Celebrities favored the intimate Tiki Room with its lavish tapa-cloth-covered walls and carved island figures. *San Francisco Chronicle* newspaper columnist Herb Caen and crooner Bing Crosby were two of the regulars at Trader Vic's.

The culinary union was very strong at the time, and Pete was a member. Bergeron hated the union and did all he could to destroy it. He really wanted an Asian to work the main bar, so one day he told Pete he was being moved back to the service bar. Pete told his boss, Mr. Chan, that he was highest on the seniority list and had worked his ass off for the front bar. He told Mr. Chan that he couldn't take it away from him. When he told him that Mr. Bergeron wanted an Asian to work the main bar, Pete turned in his resignation. He liked Mr. Chan and knew that it was hard for him to see Pete go. Mr. Chan asked him, "Pete, where you gonna go?"

"Don't worry about me, Mr. Chan," was Pete's reply. "You should worry about yourself, not me. This is my city."

He walked up the street and was hired by Mario Puccinelli, his long-time friend, at the Iron Horse on Maiden Lane.

The Iron Horse was known as a "meat market" in those days, a gathering place for financial district employees. Secretaries knew that businessmen in suits would happily buy them a drink. Abundant hors d'oeuvres were offered on the house during Happy Hour to entice pretty young women in. There was sexy energy, cheap drinks, and dinner for many of the women. It was a great pickup joint for men, who were three deep at the bar hoping to score with one of the ladies. Pete worked the day shift, which afforded very little in tips. His shift ended just when the bar began to get crowded.

Up on Broadway, Gino Del Prete and his wife, Gloria, changed the name of their new bar from House of Pisco to Gino and Gloria's. It was small, but had a most beautiful cherrywood bar that had been brought around the Horn in the mid-1800s. Gorgeously sculpted, it featured a lion head in the center of the top. The lion had a small red light bulb in his mouth. Gino had no entertainment, just a jukebox in the corner. His wife, Gloria, a beautiful and wildly popular Puerto Rican/American woman, was a local star as the "It Girl" at the Sinaloa

Cantina on Powell Street between Vallejo and Broadway, a dinner/showroom featuring Latin music and flamenco dancing. Gloria helped Gino drum up business at Gino and Gloria's when she wasn't working at the Sinaloa.

After a while, Gino took on another partner, Ernie Cunio, and changed the name to Ernie and Gino's. That partnership dissolved, and Gino became partners with Coke Infante, another North Beach rounder. Coke and Gino changed the name once again. They slathered ugly black paint on the beautiful cherry wood bar, and called the club The Black Condor.

Sam Marconi, owner of the Iron Horse, liked this kid named Tony, who was an excellent bartender. He could remember all the drink orders and hold five glasses with one hand. One day, Tony quit and Pete was given the lucrative night shift. He had worked there a year and a half by then, and felt he was ready to handle the evening rush. Pete was popular with the drinking crowd, but had to ask the waitress to repeat the drink orders once in a while, and could only hold three glasses in one hand.

Tony returned one day and asked Sam for his job back. Sam told Pete that Tony had more seniority, so he was moving Pete back to the day shift.

"He lost his seniority when he left," Pete demanded. He was used to the extra tip money—and he was pissed. Pete told Sam that if he demoted him, he would quit. Sam hired Tony anyway, so Pete quit. He walked over to Sam's Lane Club and downed a few drinks at the bar. It was there that Pete found out that everyone but him had known he was about to lose the night shift. He got real drunk and drove his new Kaiser Darrin up Columbus Avenue to The Black Condor.

Gino was sitting at the bar when Pete walked in. Pete told him he had just quit his job at the Iron Horse. He gave him all the details.

"Why don't you come and be my partner?" Gino asked Pete. He had asked Pete before on several occasions, but Pete had always declined. Pete told Gino he was too drunk to make any decisions that night. He would sleep on the idea and let him know the next day.

Pete knew Gino well enough to know that he should think seriously about this decision. But Pete was young, had been working in the bars for a few years, and figured he knew what it took to run a successful business. He was hesitant to join Gino because he was one of his party buddies. He knew that Gino was not always "minding the store." In fact, he knew that Gino was an awful businessman, but had other redeeming characteristics: he was good-looking, fun, and very popular in the North Beach scene.

Gino was "cash on delivery" for all his liquor purchases. He was in debt to the tune of around $13,000, which was lot of money in 1958. He had been cited on October 9, 1956, for filling name-brand whisky bottles with cheap knockoff liquor. He had a track record of business failures, was a heavy drinker and a partying womanizer. These were the reasons his last two partners, Coke Infante and Ernie Cuneo, had left the scene. There were many things to consider before going into business with Gino.

However, Gino was also handsome, charismatic, and could attract customers. People loved to be around Gino because it was always a great time. He had grown up in North Beach, and seemed to know everyone. Every day was a party, but if Gino took in $600 a day, he would spend $700. He was generous and often just gave away $20 or $100 bills to people he felt could use it. It wasn't long before Gino was in debt.

Pete went back to The Black Condor the next day and agreed that he would assume half of the debt, around $6,500, and become Gino's partner. Pete insisted that he would make all the business decisions and required three conditions for the deal: that Gino didn't count the cash, do any banking, or order any liquor. Gino wasn't happy with the new terms, but he didn't have much choice if he was to keep the club. They shook hands and poured a drink to seal the deal.

Down in Selma, Pietro had just made a deal to sell his grapes for $55 per ton and was ecstatic. He bought a new car and was driving it home when he suffered a heart attack and passed away on the lawn of his neighbor, Mr. Christensen, on September 9, 1957. It was a huge loss for the family as well as the community. He was very well respected in both Selma and back in San Francisco.

Angelo sold the ranch property in Selma, and Pietro's widow, Elena, moved in with her daughter, Elaine Loosigian. Angelo moved his family to Millbrae, California, and took a job at Sunset Poultry. Angelo's wife, Lillian, passed away from cancer a few years later, which left him and his teenage children, Kenny and Cheryl, devastated.

5

On the Corner
of Pee Wee Ferrari
and Lucky the Dip

The year was 1958. When Pete became partners with Gino, North Beach was the beating heart of the Italian community and San Francisco's entertainment center. Unparalleled for its fine restaurants and jumpin' jivin' nightclubs frequented not only by the locals, it was also where wild-eyed vacationing Aunt Eleanor and Uncle Fred from Milwaukee wanted to be. It was an anthill of activity, home to legendary poets, finger-snapping beatniks, and cool jazz musicians. Let's take a stroll around.

To the north of The Black Condor on Columbus was Cara's, an Italian ceramics import shop. Directly east on Broadway was La Casa, a clothing store, later called Guido Razzini's. East of La Casa was Tipsy's, a bar owned by Pee Wee Ferrari, who was fondly referred to as the "Dean" of North Beach. He was smart, and was considered an intellectual who thoughtfully attempted to answer any question you might have about life or the City. Everyone knew Pee Wee. He loved to play gin rummy, and usually had a game going on in a room above the Bank of America building on the southeast corner of Broadway and Columbus.

Pee Wee had confided to several friends that he had never seen his sweet wife, Ina, naked. That was hard to believe, and folks wondered if he also had an extramarital life, as did so many of the Broadway Boys. Pee Wee was a good friend of the California governor at the time, Edmund G. "Pat" Brown. Governor Brown's cousin later married Pee Wee's daughter. Pee Wee had connections, and was the man to call if you needed a favor of some kind.

The Roaring 20's Club, owned by Art Thanish, was next to Tipsy's. West of Roaring 20's was Pierre's, a club owned by Maurice Pierre Bessiere. Bessiere wanted to have a "nice" place where respectable urbanites could have an early evening live musical experience, and a more energetic late-night crowd that enjoyed exciting Latin dance music. He catered to the financial district's after-work crowd with unique appetizers and drinks. (Dick Boyd became his partner in 1960. Pierre's then became a sports bar, where members of the San Francisco 49ers football team liked to hang out. Most of the time the team member's drinks were served at no charge—just a nod. That was a good policy to fill the bar with bodies, but detrimental to the bottom-line profits.)

Farther east was New Joe's Restaurant, owned by Joe Engarcia and the Arrigoni brothers, Peter and Agostino, who were dual cooks and waiters. Walking into New Joe's was like arriving in Italy. The popular maître d' hotel, Frank Marino, usually welcomed you with open arms and a big smile. Regulars felt at home there, and tourists knew they had found a rare gem of a restaurant. The waiters yelled their orders across the room in their unique lingo, and served everything with extraordinary flair. Longtime waiter Emil Medina was Lebanese, but had emigrated from Mexico. He spoke seven languages—Lebanese, Spanish, Arabic, Greek, Italian, French, and English—and one would never know which language one would hear.

New Joe's was a very special restaurant where you could get a robust home-cooked Italian meal; spaghetti with meatballs, veal scaloppini, tripe, or chicken cacciatore were favorites. They served old-fashioned choices as well: savory boiled beef, pot roast, or tender liver and onions with a side of al dente spaghetti or rigatoni topped with luscious Bolognese sauce. Big chunks of chewy sourdough bread and a bowl full of butter pats accompanied all dishes.

The New Joe's burger was a one-inch-thick, hand-formed slab of juicy ground beef, charbroiled and served on a crispy sourdough roll accompanied by pepperoncini, olives, onion, lettuce, and tomato, along with fresh-cut French fries or sautéed mushrooms. Eating one of these marvels required total concentration and several napkins to catch the flavorful juices dripping from the bread. Rarely did one person finish an entire burger.

Everyone was comfortable at New Joe's. Diners sat at the counter to watch cooks banging their red-hot sauté pans on the range and tossing greens into the air, showing off their culinary skills. They loved to entertain the customers, flipping steaks, burgers, or lamb chops sizzling among the high flames of the charcoal grill. Watching them at work in the open kitchen was a remarkable show in itself.

New Joe's was where you went after a night of heavy drinking seeking to cure a mean hangover. Diners often ordered a bowl of rich *ministra maritata* soup, the classic Italian wedding soup. It consisted of broken vermicelli noodles, tiny meatballs, greens, and Parmesan cheese blended into steaming chicken broth. One never worried about calories when you needed to cure a hangover, and there were a lot of hangovers to cure.

New Joe's cooks would prepare whatever you wanted "to order." It was a late-night hangout, and one night someone wanted scrambled eggs with hamburger. He asked if the cook had anything else he could throw in, and he suggested spinach. The "Joe's Special" was born, which is still on all the "Joe's" restaurant menus and has become a well-known dish at restaurants throughout the world.

If you wanted a little privacy at New Joe's, there were several booths for dining, but for the most part the customers didn't go there for privacy. It was a place to see and be seen—to join in the action and find out what was happening in the neighborhood.

Finocchio's was next down the street, famous for its campy female impersonators who had staged shows there nightly since 1936. Finocchio's was a major stop for Gray Line's evening bus tours, bringing hundreds of tourists to watch the "decadent" drag queens. Locals supported Finocchio's, as it was a million laughs watching the sequined performers strut their stuff, singing and delivering hilarious one-liners. A little known fact is that several of the performers were straight married men with families. The job paid well and was lots of fun, so why not?

Joe Finocchio had his problems, though, with city officials, who once raided the club and arrested him for keeping a disorderly house and serving alcohol after 2 a.m. Joe settled his case in court after he agreed to run a "straight" show like a real theater, where the entertainers were not to make contact with the patrons. He pacified the Alcoholic Beverage Control by agreeing that no alcohol would be served after 2 a.m. (Joe passed away in 1986, but his wife, Eve, continued to operate Finocchio's until 1999. It was truly a "drag" when Finocchio's closed.)

West of Finocchio's was Enrico's coffee house, owned by Enrico Banducci, where the bald, black-beret-topped impresario would stroll around, playing a few squeaky strings of his violin as his form of entertainment. Enrico was friendly, had a big smile, and was very well liked by other business owners on the street. Enrico's drew an eclectic, artsy crowd who considered themselves true Bohemians as they sipped cappuccinos in front of the restaurant, a sidewalk café, for hours on end. It was a fabulous people-watching hot spot. Comedians Bill Cosby and Jonathan Winters, who were good friends of Banducci's, regularly hung out there.

Lucky Lucchesi was manager of Enrico's. Lucky had a big, gnarly, pockmarked face, which surrounded a huge bulbous nose. He could pickpocket anything from anybody at any time, hence his nickname, "The Dip." If Lucky considered you his friend, he would return the pocketed booty. If you were unlucky enough to be his adversary, he kept whatever he took.

On one occasion, Lucky tried to break up a fight between a drunken couple in the Condor Club. The woman was furious with him, and began beating Lucky with her purse. When the mêlée was over, Lucky had the man's watch and wallet, and the lady's watch and necklace. Nobody knowingly messed with Lucky.

Eric "Big Daddy" Nord, a 6-foot-7-inch hipster whom Herb Caen called the "King of the Beat Generation," rented a basement space on Jackson Street where he and his beatnik friends hung out. He called it the "hungry i." Enrico Banducci thought that it would make a great comedy nightclub spot and rented it, keeping the name.

Enrico offered some of the best entertainment at the hungry i, including comedy and folk music, giving Bill Cosby, Mort Sahl, Dick Gregory, and Lenny Bruce, to name but a few, a big leg up on their young careers. Barbara Streisand began her career there, and in 1959 the Kingston Trio recorded one of their best albums in the club, *...from the Hungry "i"* [sic].

(After the hungry i closed in 1970, Pete paid Enrico $10,000 for the name, moved the sign to the former location of Pierre's, and opened it as another topless club. Many unsuspecting tourists thought they were entering the hungry i made famous by Cosby, Bruce, and the Kingston Trio, but soon found out it was just another topless club.)

Next to the Condor was Big Al's, managed by Walter Pastore, a nephew of Victor ("Big Al") Falgiano, who was known as a pistol-packing Easterner who also carried a cane that housed a sword. (It later became a topless, and then bottomless bar.)

Further down was Vanessi's, a classy Italian restaurant with a bar usually three people deep. You could casually dine at the counter and watch the cooks at work or take a booth in the lovely dining room. Modesto Lanzoni and Bart Shea were owners. The menu featured rich veal sauté dishes such as veal picatta, scaloppini, or saltimbocca and tender osso buco a la Milanese. The chefs were experts with making pasta and flavorful sauces featuring such delicious items as spaghetti marinara, carbonara, Bolognese, or frutti di mare. The delectable ravioli and lasagna were house-made and very popular. The food at Vanessi's was some of the best in the world. You'd better be on time for your reservation in the dining room at Vanessi's or your table would be gone.

The dashing bullfighter and author Barnaby Conrad owned the El Matador nightclub at 492 Broadway. Born in San Francisco, Conrad had traveled the world and had actually fought the bulls in Spain and Mexico. He wrote a novel, *The Matador*, which sold over 3 million copies and provided enough in royalties to open the nightclub in 1953. Conrad had graduated from Yale University and was at ease among celebrities in the literary as well as the entertainment world.

Barnaby's giant colorful macaw greeted customers by introducing himself with "Hello. McGreggor here." An enormous bull's head hung on the wall. Every once in a while patrons' eyes would pop upon noticing puffs of smoke billowing from the bull's nostrils. Barnaby had hooked up a tube from the bull head to the back bar, and bartender Paul Svetkoff would delight in blowing cigarette smoke through to the bull's nostrils, which was specially distressing for the customers who had consumed a few too many.

The elegant smoke-filled room was quite small, but there was nothing small about the top-notch jazz entertainment featured inside. The house band, featured pianist John Horton Cooper and pianist/bass player Vernon Alley, often invited visiting musicians to join them onstage for jam sessions. Performers included Cal Jader, Duke Ellington, Hoagy Carmichael, and Erroll Garner.

Ann Dee operated Ann's 440 Club, a dingy lesbian hangout located at 440 Broadway. It was here that Johnny Mathis began his singing career.

On the south side of Broadway on the corner directly across the street from The Black Condor was the Bank of America. To the east of the bank was Coke Infante's bar, Coke's; Mike's Pool Hall; the Galaxy Bar, owned by Dave Rapkin; and on the next corner, another popular Italian restaurant, Swiss Louie's.

To the west on Broadway you found the Moulin Rouge, also owned by Dave Rapkin, and the Acme Theater, sometimes called The Talkies. The Purple Onion, a celebrated cellar club during the beatnik era, was on Columbus and Jackson. The Black Cat, one of The City's many gay bars, was also on Columbus down by Jackson Street.

Ernie's, the famous French restaurant, was on Kearny. Now, this is where you took a date if you really wanted to impress her or him. Ernie's—or the Blue Fox. Both restaurants were outrageously expensive, with snobby waiters who strutted through the rooms with supreme arrogance.

Voss Boreta owned the Off Broadway, a huge venue on Kearny. The Verdi movie house was on Broadway. The Liberty was a burlesque showplace where Pete's mother, fire-hoppin' mad, occasionally found her husband when they lived on Union Street.

Chinatown began at Broadway and ran south beginning at Grant, where there was a sign on the entrance of the street warning tourists and locals alike to ENTER AT YOUR OWN RISK!

Moving north along Grant Street from Broadway, you found the historic Tivoli Bar and Restaurant, a warm and comfortable restaurant/coffee house where longhaired beatniks hung out way before the Summer of Love and Haight-Ashbury phenomenon.

Further up Grant Street was Figoni's Hardware, where the shelves were stacked to the ceiling with everything imaginable. It was a central hub in the life of many North Beach residents. People could buy things there on credit, with no interest. They could leave messages there for other people. Owner Melvin Figoni had a library ladder that would slide along a rail so that he could climb up and easily retrieve whatever was requested. He provided the type of personal service that has become a thing of the past. The place was organized chaos, but he knew where everything was.

Toscano's was a clothing store on Grant Street where Pete's mother had sent him as a child to pick up socks or underwear. The Mattiolis had a charge account there, the old-fashioned kind where they just kept a running tab on a paper ledger of what was owed. A little wind-up toy dog was prominently displayed in the window, and when a penny was placed in a slot at top, it would wiggle itself until the penny was pooped out.

Iaccoppi's Butcher Shop was on the corner of Stockton and Union. Leo Rossi's parents owned it, and Big Leo worked there. Down on the corner was Rossi's Drugstore.

Looking north on Columbus and across the street one would find the Gold Spike Restaurant, operated by the Machetti family since 1920. This establishment could be considered either the best or the worst place to eat in North Beach. The food was actually pretty good, but it was a dark and greasy-looking joint that appeared dirty simply because it was so old and dingy. It seemed the décor had never been updated since it opened, and what was there had layers of grime covering it. But it was certainly a local hangout, and people felt very cool entering because they knew about it and the tourists didn't. The food was tried and true regional Italian dishes.

Lazzari's Drug Store was on Columbus Street between Broadway and Vallejo. They kept a fishbowl full of live medicinal leeches. There were lots of fistfights in North Beach, and if you received a black eye, you could go to Lazzari's, where they would stick a leech on the bruise and it would suck the blood out within a matter of five or ten minutes, turning a black bruise to a yellow bruise. You could purchase the leeches, and they were used at home as remedies for several ailments. People suffering from varicose veins brought them home and used them to extract blood. Afterward, the leeches were placed in Epsom salt, where they would disgorge their blood and be ready for more. Lazzari's was also the location where many men who suspected they had a case of the clap would get quick treatment. When the regulars walked in, the pharmacist usually knew they wanted a penicillin injection and simply said, "Pull your pants down, buddy."

Pete knew the neighborhood intimately and loved it. He had grown up there and had returned because he felt comfortable there. He wanted to put his own stamp on it, but never had any inkling of how his life and the lives of so many others would be impacted by the upcoming transformation of North Beach.

6

Becoming
the Condor

When Pete became Gino's partner in March of 1958, The Black Condor was just a small neighborhood bar with a jukebox, a bit player in the totality of what was happening in North Beach. It was popular because of its central location, relaxed ambiance, and the characters who stopped in for conversation and a drink or two. There was just barely room enough room in front of the jukebox for a couple to dance a jig on the linoleum floor. During the time that Coke Infante was a partner with Gino, Infante convinced Gino to paint the beautifully carved back bar black and pink. It looked grotesque.

The club sat 54 people and was pretty run down. Money was never spent to keep it in good repair and attractive. It looked shabby and was in desperate need of a face-lift.

Pete and Gino decided that The Black Condor needed a new name. Since one didn't pop into their heads right away, they hung a sign beside the door that said "No Name Bar" and held a contest among the customers asking them to come up with a new name. Prize money of $50 was offered for the winner. They received several suggestions, but nixed them all. A pal, Paul Jacubocci, suggested they call it the "Nothin'." "Whadaya need a name for?" he questioned.

The original Condor, 1958.

It remained the No Name Bar. They decided to give Paul the $50, and hung up a wooden picture frame with red velvet inside, indicating that it was the "Nothin' Bar." But everyone still called it The Black Condor, so eventually they gave up on a new name and decided that it should just be called the Condor.

Gino's wife, Gloria Padilla, the star of the Sinaloa Club over on Stockton Street, was wildly popular and famous in her own right. A sexy Puerto Rican beauty, Gloria had been smitten by Gino's good looks and party personality. They were married, but talk of divorce was common between them, as they were frequently quarreling and had had several public fight battles. She accused him of cheating, and he was insanely jealous of her. After a few drinks, their arguing became dreadfully violent. They were both gritty fighters, and often both sported black eyes and ugly bruises after a battle.

Chronicle columnist Herb Caen's commentary of April 29, 1957, stated, "Lovely Gloria Padilla will be out of action for a week following that battle with her husband, Gino Del Prete. Indestructible Inez Torres will replace her as the Sinaloa's headliner."

Gino was always fighting, whether with his wife, or in a brawl with one of the Condor customers. Pete recalls one particular night when Gino got in a scuffle with a guy named Tony. Gino jumped behind the bar and Tony followed him. They grabbed bottles from the back bar, hurling them through the air at each other. Pete scrambled over the bar, plunking himself between them to break it up. In the end, it was Pete who got the worst of it as his cashmere sweater, shirt, and jacket were all ripped up, and he sported a black eye himself. Off to Lazzari's Drug Store he went for the leech treatment.

It wasn't long before Gino began replacing empty whisky bottles with the cheap stuff again. He was caught in the act, and on November 2, 1958, the Condor was charged with serving inferior liquor from Canadian liquor bottles. Federal Judge George B. Harris fined the club $500, and they were placed on a one-year probation. Pete told Gino that if it ever happened again, he would just break all the premium bottles so they could not be refilled.

Other clubs in the area featured entertainment, but the Condor was too small for a live band. The jukebox was it, and they were competing with venues offering Dixieland bands, folk music, and jazz groups. Every club in the City that had a dance floor began to promote themselves as a place to dance to rock'n'roll. Freestyle solo dance crazes, such as the Hand Jive (1958), the Hully Gully (1959), and Chubby Checker's "The

Two of North Beach's most popular club owners, the flamboyant, man-about-North Beach GINO DEL PRETE (left) and the ʷˡᵘʳᵉ businesslike PETE MATTIOLI, discuss their latest club, the CHINESE PAGODA. In addition, Gino and Pete own the world famous CONDOR and MR. WONDERFUL.

Pete and Gino become partners.

Twist" (1960) were often played on the juke box at the Condor, along with blasting hits such as The Champs' "Tequila," Domenico Modugno's "Volare," and Danny & the Juniors' "At the Hop."

Pete and Gino decided to clear out a small space at the end of the bar big enough for a drum set and a couple of standing musicians. They hired a few small bands, but had a hard time competing with the larger venues. Still, it kept them in business and they began to make a little money.

In January 1960, Pete and Gino decided spend some of their holiday profits by throwing a "thank you" bash for their loyal customers. Hundreds of people tried to jam into the small club. It wasn't the free drinks and hors d'oeuvres that cost the club owners the most: by the end of the evening, they had to replace several broken glasses, some stolen bar stools, broken light fixtures, and a smashed cigarette machine. Not to mention a lawsuit from drunken patron who fell down the stairs coming from the second-level restroom.

Because the bands were set up in the tiny corner at the end of the bar next to Columbus Avenue, the music could clearly be heard from the street, which sometimes drew large crowds to the corner to listen and dance.

(One day, a few years later, Sylvester Stewart, a DJ at KSOL, a radio station playing the latest soul sounds, walked in and asked if he could play there. A good-looking and talented kid, Pete hired him for a few gigs and discovered that he was not only proficient on the guitar, but played excellent keyboard, drums, and bass. He didn't have a fully formed band at the time and was paid only $15 per night. Soon calling himself "Sly Stone," he hung out at the Condor along with Bobby Freeman and other black singers of the time. He eventually formed his band, "Sly and the Family Stone," moving on to bigger gigs in L.A. and elsewhere, becoming a huge R&B/funk music star with such hits as "Dance to the Music." Sly often stopped by the Condor during his career to check out the action.)

At lunchtime, a table was placed where the band played at night. Sandwiches and hofbrau items were prepared and served from that table during the day. Businessmen and their secretaries frequently stopped by for a bite and a "two martini" lunch.

One night, Frank Domano, a Condor bar regular, fell down the stairs in a drunken stupor, banging his body up pretty good. A couple of days later, George Berrafato, another bar fixture, commented that he hadn't seen Frank around, and asked Pete if he had seen him. Pete, who knew that Frank lived in the Chez Dante Hotel above the club, said, "No, maybe he's up in his hotel room." They found Frank in his bed in a coma. They put cold towels on his face and called the doctor, who diagnosed him with spinal meningitis. The doctor made Pete and George get vaccinated for the disease. Frank passed away three days after falling down the stairs.

Frank had a brother nicknamed PDQ ("Pretty Darned Quick," a name given him for his quick hand at picking up money left on the bar by unsuspecting patrons). PDQ wanted to initiate a lawsuit against the Condor for Frank's death. Later it was discovered that he died from a tumor that had formed in his brain after a car accident in which he rolled his Volkswagen. Joe Engarcia later barred PDQ from the cocktail lounge at New Joe's for stealing cash off the bar.

When Pete was twenty-eight, he decided it was time to get married and start a family. There were plenty of beautiful ladies at the club competing for Pete's attention, but an attractive secretary a couple years his senior caught his eye. She was newly divorced, with a seven-year-old son from a previous marriage, but there was something about her he especially liked. Pete married Arlene Weir in 1959 and adopted her son, Chris.

For his wedding and reception, Pete rented the South End Rowing Club, located adjacent to Aquatic Park. He decided that to save money, he and his friends would prepare all the food themselves. Since there was no kitchen in the Condor, Pete asked the owners of the El Cid across the street if they could use their kitchen to prepare the wedding dinner.

Pete worked feverishly, slicing roast beef, turkey, and Italian cold cuts for trays. A Condor regular, Lucky Lucchessi, took charge of boiling the spaghetti and making the Bolognaise sauce. Other friends loaded their vehicles with food and hauled it to the Rowing Club.

"Hey, Pete, it's time for the wedding!" Lucky yelled at Pete, as he sweated over some sliced salami.

"Oh shit, Arlene will be furious," Pete shouted, as he removed his apron and revealed his Italian-made wedding suit. He checked his pocket and discovered his money clip was missing.

"Lucky, you son of a bitch! Give me my poke!"

Lucky, grinning from ear to ear, handed over the fat billfold and told Pete to get on with the wedding.

The wedding was a huge party, crashed by anyone and everyone that Pete, Arlene, and even Gino had ever met. In the end, it was thought that over 700 people stopped by to eat, drink, and congratulate the couple.

Married life was difficult for the couple, as anyone can imagine. Pete had to transition from a single swinger to instant father of a handsome young blond boy. He took Chris to the Elks club often, and taught him how to swim and swing at a boxing bag. He spent as much time as he could with the boy, relishing the role of new father.

Arlene quit her secretary job when they married. She hated the hours Pete had to work, as sometimes Pete didn't get home until 3 or 4 in the morning.

On many occasions, Pete had heard his father's stories of life in his hometown of Sassoferrato. Pietro spoke only Italian in the home, so Pete conversed with him in Italian, but sometimes answered him in English. Pietro corresponded with his brother in Italy through an occasional letter.

When Pete's mother, Elena, had recovered somewhat from Pietro's death, Pete decided to take her, Arlene, and Chris to visit Sassoferrato. An uncle, Pietro's brother Giovanni, and his wife, Ignesa, were still living on the little hillside farm where Pietro grew up.

They flew into Rome, rented a car, and drove east towards the Adriatic Sea along the ancient Roman route, the Via Flaminia. Upon arriving in the Marche district, they discovered the small farming village of Sassoferrato, a town brimming with Roman artifacts and history. They asked some locals if they knew Giovanni Mattioli and were told to follow a small gravel road to the top of the hill. They passed several small farmhouses along the way and upon seeing each one, Elena cried out, "*O, Dio cane!* I hope this isn't it." It was a very poor area.

At the top of the hill they came upon the last house. "Uh, I guess this must be it," Elena stated drearily. It was a typical Italian farmhouse, with chickens running all around and two oxen poking their heads out of a cavern dug under the house. An old woman wearing a scarf was gathering eggs, and looked up to see who was there. Pete got out of the car walked over to her, just as two Italian fighter jets flew over. The woman shook her fist in the air, cursing the airplanes and screaming, "*Dio cane*, you make too much noise!" (In Italian)

Turning to Pete, she asked, "Can I help you?"

Pete said, "I'm Pietro's son. The brother of Giovanni."

Ignesa's eyes rolled back as she gasped and collapsed to the ground. Just then, Giovanni came out from under the house yelling, "What's going on? Who are you?" He ran towards Ignesa.

Pete said, "I'm Pietro's son, your brother's son."

Giovanni shook Ignesa and was able to bring her back from her fainting spell. She sat up. Then he walked over to Pete, shook his hand and gave him a big hug. "*Benvenuto!*" he bellowed.

His uncle and aunt immediately set about fixing a dinner for their guests. They began by grabbing a chicken and wringing its neck, killing it instantly. Then they threw it into a huge pot of boiling water, which loosened the feathers. Giovanni plucked the bird, throwing the feathers into a newspaper and discarding them. Then he gutted the bird, butchered it into sizeable pieces, and placed them into a simmering tomato *sugo*. While he was preparing the bird, Ignesa was busy with flour and eggs, making fresh pasta. After each task, the cooks washed their hands and showed them to their guests as if to prove how clean they were with their work.

The meal was absolutely delicious, and the family thoroughly enjoyed meeting their relatives. When they were ready to leave, Pete pulled out a wad of money and handed it to Giovanni, who adamantly refused to take it, but, after a few nudges from Ignesa, finally slipped it into his pocket.

On the way down the hill, their bellies full, Elena declared, "The *sugo* was delicious, but that chicken must have been a hundred years old! That's the toughest old bird I've ever tried to eat."

When Pete and Arlene arrived back in San Francisco, they found out that Arlene was pregnant with their daughter, Amy. Pete had always wanted children, so this was delightful news. Amy Elena Mattioli was born on October 29, 1960. Pete was excited about the birth of his beautiful brown-eyed daughter, and vowed to spend some quality time with her.

7

The Remodel

In 1961, Cara's, an Italian ceramics import company just to the north of the Condor on Columbus Avenue, moved to another location, vacating the space. Pete and Gino jumped at the opportunity to take it over, and signed a lease for it. They began plans to expand their little bar.

They hired Doug Dunn, an ex–football player turned contractor, to draw up some remodel plans for the club. They decided on four brick arches for the front of the building facing Columbus Street. Folding doors that were constructed inside the arches could be opened to the street, which created a sidewalk café impression although patrons were still seated inside the club.

Cara's had two 12-foot-by-12-foot, half-inch-thick plate glass display windows facing Columbus Avenue. These would have to be removed to begin construction on the fourth brick arch. Pete noticed some window guys working up the street at Luigi's Pizza. He and Gino walked up and asked if they would like to take the windows from Cara's and keep them for free. The window worker walked down to take a look and noted the hundreds of screws holding the windows in place. He told them no, he didn't want the windows, and if Pete and Gino wanted them removed, they would have to pay to have them taken out.

"Us pay you?" Pete screamed. "You're crazy! These are expensive windows!"

Furious, Pete went back to the Condor and discussed what had just happened. Gino spotted some loose bricks in the corner of Cara's, and then looked at Pete. Almost instantaneously, they picked up the bricks and hurled them at the windows, shattering them and the calm of the entire neighborhood. Glass shards flew all over the sidewalk, causing pedestrians to shriek in horror. Broken glass sailed out onto Columbus Avenue, stopping traffic and causing pandemonium. Policemen were on the scene within a minute demanding the two crazy young Italians sweep up the mess immediately. The police cordoned off the street with barriers. Pete and Gino spent the next four hours cleaning up their mess. This might be about the time the proprietors of the Blue Fox and other North Beach businesses began calling them "the kids on the corner." That image stuck to them for years.

As part of the remodel, they punched a hole in the wall dividing the two businesses and began removing the sheetrock between the beams. There was a tiny storeroom on the left of the main door as you entered the club. They removed it, made a little alcove, and eventually placed seating there.

They discovered a huge horizontal beam made of several laminated two-by-six boards. Pete and Gino decided it was in the way and had to be removed. Pete grabbed a saw and began to slice away at the beam. After he had cut through three or so of the boards he heard several loud cracks. The remaining boards were bending, and he realized that he was carving through one of the main support beams for the two-story Dante Hotel located above the club.

The ceiling was coming down; they were jeopardizing the integrity of the entire building and putting many lives at risk. Pete called the City administrators, who quickly dispatched a crew, who inserted a jack to hold the building up while a new beam was built, inserted the new beam, and let the building back down to rest on the reconstructed support beam. Once again, the two crazy Italian kids had lucked out and a disaster was averted.

An elevated stage was built along the north wall, a real stage that accommodated larger entertainment groups, with room for go-go dancers as well. Drapes were hung, covering the back wall behind the stage.

They pasted red-and-gold flocked wallpaper on the walls of the club, giving it a seductive, boudoir look. Pete ordered cocktail tables with black wrought iron stands and Carrara marble tops from Italy. Gold-lacquered soda fountain chairs were tucked around the tables. Red-and-gold carpeting with a fleur-de-lis design was laid throughout the club. Four beautiful Spanish chandeliers illuminated from the ceiling, creating a warm, elegant ambiance.

The back bar was an antique with fine detail, exquisitely hand-carved from cherrywood, with a lion's head adorning the top, in whose mouth a small red lightbulb glowed. The unique bulb had a huge piece of carbon inside, insuring it a very long life. Pete remembered the beauty of the bar's original finish and hated the ugly black and pink paint job that had been applied while Coke Infante was a partner. He hired an elderly Italian craftsman named Ralph to restore the bar to its original appearance.

Ralph worked for over a month using dental tools, painstakingly removing the thick black and pink paint. The results were amazingly beautiful. The bar looked like new; the lustrous cherrywood gleamed through the new varnish.

When the restoration was complete, Pete met with Ralph to pay him. Pete noticed that the red light bulb in the lion's mouth was missing. When he asked Ralph where it was, Ralph began to cry. He had placed the bulb in his pocket for safekeeping and had forgotten about it. He dropped a tool into the same pocket, breaking the bulb. Ralph had shopped every hardware store in the City trying to find a replacement bulb, but was unsuccessful. The electrical system was very old and would have to be completely rewired to accommodate a new bulb, so the little red light bulb in the lion's mouth was never replaced and is still missing today.

A beautiful old cappuccino machine sat on the bar. It made delicious cappuccino, but created such a racket while brewing that it frightened the bartenders. They thought it might blow up any minute, and finally it actually did! It blew coffee out a hole and made a big mess on the bar. They had to take it out.

The club's restrooms were located upstairs, and the stairs had a hand-rail attached to the wall but were open on the other side. When Pete was dumping some construction debris at the salvage yard, he spotted an old bannister that he thought might work for the staircase in the club. He paid $30 for it, and it was a perfect fit.

Pete called Lori DeGracia, who owned Alpha Distributing, a liquor supply company. Lori owned the sole rights for distribution of Tuaca, a very popular liqueur imported from Italy. Pete had become friends with Lori and his father while working at previous bars. Lori liked Pete and asked what he needed.

"About $40,000 worth of liquor," Pete replied.

"What?" Lori shrieked. "How do you plan to pay for it?"

"Well, we spent so much on our remodel that I don't have money to pay for it now. But when I sell this booze, I'll pay you—and then I'll borrow $40,000 more," Pete stated confidently.

Lori trusted him, and within a few days truckloads of liquor were delivered to the Condor. They unloaded it, and carried box after box upstairs to the storage area. Before long, they noticed that one of the structural beams was beginning to bend from the weight of the liquor. Once again, the Chez Dante Hotel was sagging and beginning to collapse into the club.

"Take it down!" Pete yelled. "Get those boxes back downstairs, the building is ready to collapse!" They quickly went upstairs carried all the boxes two flights down to the basement for storage.

Dunn's mother actually owned the construction company, and when it came time to pay her for the contracting services, there was no money. She would pester her son, who would tell Pete, "Hey, can't you give me some money for my mom? She won't leave me alone." They paid what they could, but would usually pacify Mr. Dunn with a few free drinks. Eventually they paid her in full.

On November 9, 1961, Pete and Gino threw a big grand opening party and invited all of San Francisco to come see their new hofbrau restaurant and nightclub. They dressed their cocktail waitresses in gold lamé jumpsuits and prepared for the party. Gino said the girls looked like I. Magnin paratroopers. Free food and drinks were served throughout the night to a boisterous crowd. They knew they had a winner, though, and made that judgment by the number of beautiful women who attended the opening.

Painters Walter and Margaret Keane stopped by often for sandwiches and a beer served at the new hofbrau. Comedian Lenny Bruce, who lived in an upstairs apartment on Broadway, also stopped in frequently.

Actor Vincent Edwards, television's Dr. Ben Casey, once decked one of the Condor patrons who wouldn't leave him alone at the club. "I'm just like you," Edwards had told the young man. "Leave me alone." Coke Infante was hanging out at the Condor at the time and asked the young man to leave. He refused, and threw a right towards Casey. Casey responded by blocking the swing and landing his right fist into the kisser of the young man. Coke picked him up and threw him out.

Chronicle columnist Herb Caen was a regular at the Condor and mentioned the club often in his writings throughout the '60s and '70s. Some samples:

> Last of the Beatniks: It looked like old times a couple of moons ago at the Condor where a young Zen mother in a leotard, with her hair down to there, relaxed at the bar, feeding beer to her young baby. The tot seemed to be taking it well and besides "There's nothing like burping a baby after he's had a little beer. You get a REAL burp." Uh-huh.

> Sal Mineo (fine in *Exodus*) wandered into the Condor at Columbus and B'way, whereupon owner Gino Del Prete remembered that Mike's Pool Hall, across the street, had a Mineo record in its jukebox. He dashed over there, called a repairman to unlock the box, snatched the record, and galloped back—all in vain. Sal had wandered on.

> Sometimes it pays to pub crawl. If you'd happened to wander into the Condor Tuesday night, you'd have heard Tony Bennett (in person) singing his hot hit, "I Left My Heart in San Francisco," in answer to the pleas of the mob. Then he walked outside to find that S.F had done something for HIM: a tag on his car.

A write-up in the May 1962 *This Month in San Francisco*, a pocket guide to the City's entertainment said:

> Gino Del Prete and Pete Mattioli's intimate and jiving nightclub located at the crossroads of the City's nightlife . . . one of San Francisco's busiest corners, where show-folk, celebrities, and other interesting characters of the active set congregate. This is the only sidewalk nightclub in town. Entertainment provided nightly by the Gary David Trio, a hard-swinging combo featuring lovely Jo Ryder, an outstanding vocalist.

One night, while singing a dramatic version of "Angel Eyes" with her eyes closed, Ryder's dress strap slipped off her shoulder. As it fell down, the crowd reacted with *pssssts* and hisses to alert her, but it was too late. The strap fell down, down, and way below her braless bosom: a possible preview to what would happen three years later?

Pete booked a Dean Martin lookalike, Tino Gerin, who performed on the new stage to a packed Condor audience. Bebe Sherman, a dynamic singing comedienne, and vocalist Vicki Fraser performed with the Jesters, the Condor house band. Singers Tudy Buchart and Nancy Styles also kept things lively in the club. Pete and Gino would travel to Los Angeles, Las Vegas, and Miami to book groups for the Condor.

It was a constant search for exciting entertainment to showcase on their new stage. Bobby Freeman, who had written and had recorded the huge hit "Do You Wanna Dance?" in 1958, was booked into the Condor frequently during the early 1960s. He rocked the crowd night after night.

Sylvester Stewart, who by then had taken the name Sly Stone, hung out at the Condor to catch Bobby Freeman's performances. In 1964, Stewart, working for Autumn Productions, helped produce an album for Bobby, which included the hit song, "Come On and Swim." This recording revitalized Freeman's career and launched "The Swim," which became a wildly popular dance craze, with dancers making swimming moves, breaststrokes and backstrokes, with their arms, holding their noses, and bending their knees like they were going under water. Bobby performed it on Dick Clark's *American Bandstand* and *Shindig*.

Across the street at the Off Broadway supper club, Mel Tormé, headlined, with dancing nightly until 1 a.m. Bimbo's, another popular supper club on lower Columbus Avenue, featured the Eddie Belasco Trio and others.

Dave Rapkin owned the Moulin Rouge, which was accepted as a "dignified" strip club. One of the exotic dancers who performed at the Moulin Rouge, Sandy Loren, was quoted in the September 18, 1963, edition of the *San Francisco Chronicle*:

> "I don't care what they call it. I'm a strip teaser. I don't dance around with flowers in my teeth. And, this isn't the Garden of Eden." She continued, "You take some guy from a small town somewhere. He's a big man there. And you give him a couple of drinks and he thinks he's a big man here. You can see him coming rooty-toot-toot." Miss Loren, who has learned some holds from a wrestler friend, has a ready response for the small town Lotharios. "I punch 'em right in the nose."
>
> Oddly enough, some men brought their wives to watch the show at the Moulin Rouge. They frequently provide a hostile audience, Miss Loren had discovered. "A woman looks at me as if to say, 'You can't have my husband, you hussy.' That's a laugh! I need their fat, bald little husbands like a third head."

Down the street at Bimbo's 365 Club, the girls admitted that they were regularly getting notes backstage from patrons who would like to meet up. Vicki Tregoning, a stately and beautiful twenty-year-old showgirl, confided, "It's usually taboo for any of us to join the customers."

The Condor became a hub of activity during the day, serving sandwiches and drinks to the business crowd, and morphing into the hottest nightclub in town at night, offering entertainment seven nights a week. They served hofbrau fare from 11 a.m. to 8 p.m. and from 2 a.m. to 4 a.m. They had a 2:30 a.m. show, but were not allowed to serve alcohol after 2 a.m. The city's swankiest socialites, artists, musicians, and street characters frequented it. The busy nightclub owners dressed in three-piece custom suits made with beautiful Italian fabric, white shirts with button-down collars adorned with expensive cufflinks, perfectly looped skinny ties, and polished Florsheim shoes. The female patrons wore daring cocktail dresses, beautiful jewelry, high heels, and fur coats to ward off the chilly fog of San Francisco.

Pete and Gino open the doors to the newly remodeled Condor nightclub, 1961.

8

Big Davey

Pete met Davey Rosenberg in 1962 when he and some of his buddies began hanging out in the Broadway clubs. A San Francisco native, Davey grew up in the Richmond District. His father owned a kosher butcher shop on Fillmore Street. Davey played football for Lowell High School, but never excelled scholastically. He tried City College and San Francisco State, but quickly dropped his college aspirations. He hated school, and figured he was smart enough succeed on his own.

Davey Rosenberg. Big Davey Rosenberg. Big Davey. Fat Davey. Everyone in North Beach seemed to know the fast-talking, street-savvy Big Fat Davey. Davey had a huge appetite for the good things in life, one of which was food. He imposed an enormous figure on the street, weighing somewhere between 350 and 400 lbs. He had a great sense of humor, and was very well liked. When Davey entered a room, everyone knew he was there, as his body filled up a large part of it. Davey knew what was happening in each and every nightclub in town, and decided he wanted to work in the business. He took up cigar smoking, bought a big convertible, and began telling people that he was a public relations agent. People believed him, and soon he had made a business for himself.

Competition was intense up and down the street, with every club owner looking for the newest twist on entertainment, sometimes stealing groups from each other. Most of the bands were rock'n'roll, folk, or soul, with go-go girls wearing miniskirts and white boots dancing on stage next to the musicians.

Pete hired Davey, the hulking newly titled talent scout, press- and public relations agent to find and book entertainment for the Condor. Soon afterward, Davey was successful in convincing other club owners in North Beach of his talents. Davey Rosenberg became the man of the hour on the street. If you wanted to know what was grooving, just ask Davey.

Davey took over booking most of the entertainment and publicity at the Condor, which he was very good at. Often he called newspaper columnists like Dick Nolan, Stanton Delaplane, or Herb Caen to let them know what was happening on the Broadway Strip. And publish it they did.

Pete, Gino, and Davey Rosenberg traveled to other cities to find rock'n'roll groups to change out with the house band, Jokers Three, and keep the entertainment exciting. They went to Oakland, the Peninsula, San Jose, and Seattle looking for the hottest singers. They flew to Los Angeles to watch Johnny Rivers perform at the Whisky a Go Go on Sunset Strip, and hired him to play an extended gig. Tino Gerin, a sensational vocalist who had appeared at the Fontainebleau in Miami Beach and Mr. Kelly's in Chicago, performed frequently at the club. The Righteous Brothers dropped in often to sing with whatever band was playing, although were never formally hired by the Condor. Sometimes Davey's ads for the Condor would proclaim their entertainers had arrived "Direct from Las Vegas" or "Direct from Miami Beach," whether that was true or not.

While Pete was handling most management aspects of the club, ordering liquor, hiring and firing, counting the cash, and depositing it at the Bank of America across the street, Davey was busy booking groups and setting the performance schedules. Gino more or less assumed the life of Riley, drinking, playing liar's dice (he was very good at concealing his little finger while it flipped the dice), picking up his paycheck—and women at the club. He traveled with Pete to Vegas and Los Angeles to

Davey Rosenberg and unknown dancer.

check out entertainment, but was not involved in the day-to-day operation of the club.

While staying at the Sands in Las Vegas, Pete and Gino met up
with members of the famous "Rat Pack": Frank Sinatra, Peter Lawford,
Sammy Davis, Jr., and (Bing's son) Lindsay Crosby in the foggy steam
room of the hotel. After exchanging a few tall tales, they decided they
would party together.

On July 22, 1963, Pete came to work and found the Condor safe open and the safe door missing. Police were called in to investigate. The burglars got away with $6,781 in cash. The case was never solved, but especially puzzling was the missing safe door. The police said that it was probably an inside job.

Davey made sure the Condor was getting its share of press. Monique Benoit, a *San Francisco Chronicle* writer, interviewed Gino. Their conversation was published in the November 15, 1963, edition:

"Me, I want to retire by the time I am 40," said the 32-year-old man, sipping his second cognac, which he was having instead of lunch.

"You mean you would get out of a business you love so much?" I asked Gino Del Prete, co-owner of the Condor Café in North Beach.

"No chance. What I want is enough money to own places without having to run them. Now I don't tend bar anymore, so at night, I wander around the place, drink with the people, talk, and drop in the neighborhood places to check the action and have a ball. I love nightlife."

"This sounds like an easy life."

"Listen, sweetheart (I was making points). I have worked hard for over 20 years, don't kid yourself. At seven, I used to get up at 4 a.m. to help out my father in his ravioli factory. See those muscles? They got hard lifting and carrying bags from the time I was ten."

"Why didn't you take over the ravioli business, which was already there?" I asked Gino, who eight years ago opened the Condor without a cent to his name and has since made it into one of the hottest spots in North Beach.

"No chance. Me, I like the glamour of the bar nightclub business. You can dress real sharp. It's hip. It's fast—you go, go, go all the time," said Gino, who looks like a tough guy in an Italian picture, ready to pick a fight and ready to take in stray dogs.

"Do you always drink like this?" I asked him when he was ordering his fourth cognac.

"In this business, you've got to drink, you've got to create an atmosphere, and you've got to be right in with your customers. Why do you think people come to a bar? Not for relaxation. They want excitement, men want to meet women, women want to meet men. They want noise, music, and life, and you've got to give it to them. I love people, the good and the bad. Take the hookers, for instance, you've got to read them. They have their own code of ethics, and they are more loyal than so-called good people. Give a hooker a fifty, you can be sure you'll get it back."

"Aren't there people who take advantage of you with hard-luck stories, though?"

"Sure, I don't mind them. If a bum comes and asks for a quarter, I may give him a buck."

"Why do you do that?"

"Honey, some people can't work; they were born helpless, and lazy, and don't know how to get along in the world. Anyway, I figure I have done many wrong things in my life, and it's my way of doing a little right."

"What about the girls?" I asked Gino, who looks like a swinger. (I learn fast.)

"Well, what about them? I can read them. Anyway, I am a married man with a 20-month-old baby girl. I spoil her rotten. My wife is a dancer. We have been married for several years. She comes from Puerto Rico and she understands life, thank God. I wouldn't have married an all-American girl for all the tea in China. They know nothing of life.

"Me, I am a gambler. I like to shake dice with friends or play poker all night. Sometimes I don't go home for two or three days. I call my wife so she won't worry. Maybe I am a little goofy, but honey, I am alive," said Gino ordering another cognac.

"I've got to go, Gino."

"All right, doll. You know, you are OK," said Gino, getting up and kissing me like an old friend. I felt like I had made the grade.

Chronicle columnist Ron Fimrite, wrote in September 1963, "It was Tuesday night in the Condor, a remarkably raucous tavern at Broadway and Columbus, which has achieved a certain eminence in North Beach as 'the place where all the action is.' The bar was peopled alternately by painted young things in beehive hairdos and lean and hungry men." He further lamented about the price of a drink, costing $1.25, with a two-drink minimum. He wrote that even a teetotaler could easily drop $20 for a night of fun in North Beach. 'But,' he said, 'there are girls, girls, girls.'"

Stepping into the Condor from a cold and foggy street on a typical Saturday night was "wild, man, I mean swingin'," wrote *Chronicle* columinist Merla Zellerbach. She continued:

> Before attempting any description of the goings on, however, let me outline some of the characters: first, there's Gino, co-owner and King of the Twist, and his partner, Pete, a quieter type. Then there's Hommy, the dapper-dressed midget; Carol, the curvy cocktail waitress of the white leotard and black stockings; Fong, the bald-headed Chinese man, who wanders in nightly, speaks to no one, circles the tables, and leaves; and Remo, the handsome bouncer, who never changes his facial expression. As the curtain rises, my husband and I enter the premises, Remo gazes into the distance, Carol waves and wiggles a hip. On stage, "The Jesters" are giving it everything, stomping twisting grinding out rhythm. Gino appears and sits down at our table.
>
> "Music's kinda loud tonight, isn't it?" I say.
>
> "The louder the beat, the more people drink," he answers. An Oriental walks by and Gino yells, "Hey, I killed your brother?"
>
> (He is recalling the internecine war of his youth, when any Chinese who ventured north of Broadway literally risked his neck.) Fong stares straight ahead, makes his rounds, and leaves.
>
> The music gets louder and wilder and Carol finds herself atop the piano doing a frenzied twist. Walter Keane comes over from the bar, lifts Hommy under one arm, carries him struggling and kicking to the piano, and sets the midget down beside the waitress. Carol and Hommy twist madly, and the audience screams and applauds. "I killed your brother!" yells Gino to Fong, who has made his second and final appearance.

As the curtain falls, Remo is standing by the doorway, adjusting his earplugs. He isn't anti-social at all. He just can't stand the noise.

Gino drove around town in a shiny new red Cadillac convertible, and Pete bought a green and white Cadillac Coupe deVille. They had their choice of San Francisco's most beautiful women. Two good-looking young Italians, sporting new cars and with fists full of dollars to flash around, they were living the fast life and seeing their dreams come true.

Of course, the two were both married and seemingly had the best of both worlds. That was far from the truth, as their home life was anything but tranquil. Gino fought constantly with Gloria, publicly and privately, about infidelity. Their fights were very physical, with both receiving hateful blows and bloodied faces. Since Gloria lived in the City and had a dancing career of her own, she heard about and saw firsthand the raw truth of Gino's cheating.

Pete and Arlene argued about cheating as well, and about the discipline of their children. Arlene felt isolated. She loved San Francisco and missed being a part of the action in the City. Pete was of the old school, and believed his wife should tend to the home and children. One morning, he was driving home after sunup when he saw his six-year-old daughter, Amy, walking to school on her own. He picked her up and noticed the rips in her leotards. Her hair was uncombed and her face unwashed. When he arrived back home with her, he discovered his wife, Arlene, still in bed with a huge hangover. Amy had gotten herself up to get ready for school by herself. There was burned toast in the toaster.

Pete got a bucket, filled it with cold water, and threw it at Arlene, who was still in the bed. Another huge fight ensued, with both accusing each other of infidelity. Pete stitched up Amy's stockings and took her to school. Then he went home to bed and tried to ease his own massive hangover.

9

George and Teddy

The Condor house band at the time was called Jokers Three. Tom Carter played guitar; David Sartuche, Sr., played bass; and Jerry Martini, who later performed with Sly and the Family Stone, was the saxophonist. Roger Serao on the drums. They were all excellent musicians in their own right, and played whatever they heard on the radio or jukebox: rock'n'roll, jazz, rhythm-and-blues. Anything with a beat.

Sometime in 1962, a young black singer named George Hamilton began dropping into the Condor to check out the action. During the band's breaks, George mingled with them and told them he sang. George was from the Bay Area, but was immersed in the new soul and rhythm-and-blues sounds emitting from Motown. One night, they invited George to sing with them. Seizing the chance, George hopped up on the stage and the crowd screamed its approval. He definitely had "it."

George's friend Teddy Brown, a black man who had grown up in Detroit, Michigan, started hanging with Hamilton at the club. George asked Teddy to join him onstage, and there was immediate chemistry between them. They knew they had something special—if only their act would be accepted. The Jokers were Caucasian, but mixed-race groups

George and Teddy with the Jokers Three and singer Trini Lopez.

were becoming more common. Soul music was quickly defining the music of the 1960s, and they wanted to be part of it.

The young singers were given a few nights a week for their show, but soon became headliners at the club, singing such hits as "Bye Bye, Love," "Rockin' Robin," and "Yakity Yak." According to John L. Wasserman, a reporter at the *San Francisco Chronicle*, they became phenomenally successful within a one-year span. Wasserman wrote that "they were virtually unknown until singing at the Condor, and within 18 months, they (A) made the club into one of the four biggest money-making night spots in San Francisco, (B) entertained a host of celebrities attracted by the driving cacophony, including Frank Sinatra, Billy Daniels, and Kim Novak, (C) been signed by Reprise-Warner Brothers to a long-term recording contract, (D) become the protégés of Phil Harris, (E) signed for numerous night club and television appearances, and (F) survived all this with a minimum loss of composure or increase in hat size."

In the Wasserman interview, George and Teddy both agreed that their lives had "changed from days of uncertainty to looking pretty good." Teddy pointed at Davey Rosenberg and said, "I'll tell you how success has changed my life: I met Dave Rosenberg."

Wasserman continued, "Rosenberg modestly lowered his eyes and scuffled his feet on the floor. Then, reflecting, he stated that, 'If you print that, I'll sue you for libel. And remember, it's spelled R_O_S_E_N_B_E_R_G.'"

At the heart of their show were current top-40 songs, familiar to their audience, but they sang these songs with such passion and soul they made them their own, songs such as "What'd I Say?" made famous by Ray Charles and "If I Had a Hammer," written by Pete Seeger and made famous by Trini Lopez and Peter Paul and Mary. They sang Beatles songs like "I Want to Hold Your Hand," giving it a definite rhythm-and-blues flavor. George and Teddy packed the house singing songs that were well known to their audience and had the entire club singing, dancing, screaming, and sweating.

The word spread quickly about George and Teddy's show, the hottest act in town. Celebrities began dropping in to check them out. Janis Joplin, trying to form a band, was organizing jam sessions at a ski shop down the street. She loved coming into the Condor to catch George and Teddy's act. Sonny Charles, lead singer of The Checkmates, Lenny Bruce, Robert Mitchum, Walter Keane, and Victor Mature were regulars. George once spotted Ann Margaret in the audience and invited her to the stage to sing with them. Ann was thrilled at the chance to sing and dance with George and Teddy! George Hamilton, the actor, sat at the Condor bar several nights when he was in town. Sylvester "Sly Stone" Stewart was a good friend of the duo, and dropped by the Condor often. Truman Capote enlivened the scene at the Condor when he stopped in to do the Twist to George and Teddy's beat.

Trini Lopez appeared regularly at the Off Broadway Club across the street from the Condor. He was a steady customer at the Condor, as he had fallen hard for Terry "Torchie" Brockman, a gorgeous young woman who won "Miss Cocktail Waitress of 1963" at the Condor.

The Condor became a top hangout for the sports world's players, San Francisco 49ers as well as the San Francisco Warriors basketball team stars Wilt Chamberlain and Nate Thurmond. San Francisco

Scopitone, the first video jukebox.

Giants players Willie Mays, Willie McCovey, Bobby Bonds (Barry's father), Dusty Baker, and more checked out the action regularly. Boxer Eddie Machin and George became quite good friends. They came to see the show, but they knew the hottest ladies also frequented the Condor.

The Scopitone Jukebox, invented in Europe in the late 1950s but not sold in the U.S. until the early 1960s. featured a 16mm video and soundtrack of an artist's performance shown on a screen at the top of the machine. It sold for $3,500, a steep price, but Pete and Gino thought it a good investment for the club. George and Teddy made a video (surrounded by go-go girls doing the Swim!) of "Ain't That Just Like Me" for the Scopitone. The video is a classic and can be found on YouTube. Although the Scopitone was never a financial success, many consider it as the original version of MTV.

In 1963, George and Teddy recorded a live album on Mammoth Records called *The Condor!*. They closed the club to the public and allowed only a few friends inside during the recording. Tom Donohue, the popular DJ at KYA Radio, wrote on the album cover:

> The boys have been working together only about two years but they mesh like the gears of a fine watch in a synchronized effort that couldn't be bettered by Siamese twins. In addition, they get a top-flight backing from the Jokers Three—each a capable soloist in his own right and as a group capable of working with singers rather than against them—a rare talent for

accompanists. George and Teddy can do all your old favorites and the new ones too—and nine times out of ten make them sound better than the originals! The Condor is always crowded, but somehow hosts Gino Del Prete and Pete Mattioli always find room for a couple more. The enticingly clad waitresses are equally adept with trays or table-top twisting, and an occasional customer gets sufficiently carried away to join George or Teddy on stage for a little Hully Gully or Mashed Potatoes.

By early 1964, George and Teddy and the Jokers Three had established themselves as the Condor house band/entertainment and were outrageously popular. Although Davey booked them into other venues in Las Vegas and Los Angeles, their home was the Condor. They decided to change their stage name officially to George and Teddy and the Condors. Under their new name, they were first act to perform at the opening of Nero's Nook at Caesar's Palace in Las Vegas, and later they played at the Frontier Hotel.

Davey arranged for them to record an album in Los Angeles for Reprise Records, a record company formed by Frank Sinatra, *George and Teddy and the Condors: In Person from Ciro's Le Disc*. While there, they were introduced to Sonny Bono, of Sonny and Cher. The executive from Reprise told Pete that Sonny was going to A & R the new recording. (A & R, or Artists and Repertoire, is responsible for scouting talent and the subsequent artistic and commercial development of musicians.) Pete refused to work with Sonny, citing his youth, inexperience, and sloppy appearance. Pete didn't like his long hair and hippie attire; another promoter was hired for George and Teddy's album. (Thirty years later, that "longhaired hippie" was elected to the U.S. House of Representatives as a Republican!)

Later that year, Pete met Sonny again, this time with his wife, Cher, backstage at the Hyatt Music Theater, later known as the Circle Star Theatre in Burlingame. They were opening for George and Teddy. Pete considered booking them at the Condor, but decided not to. Six months later, Sonny and Cher recorded "I've Got You, Babe," which launched their career into the stratosphere.

George and Teddy wore beautiful tailor-made suits, skinny ties, and polished shoes for their act. The Condor footed the bill for most of their clothing, which they regularly purchased from Vince Correnti's shop on Kearny Street, where Johnny Mathis also shopped. One day after picking up several new suits, George and Teddy decided to go to breakfast. They left all the suits in the back seat of George's convertible while they went to eat. When they returned they saw that all the suits were gone. George remembers having to tell Pete that all the suits were stolen from his car. Pete was furious.

In 1965, an entertainment promoter who was friends with an Italian nightclub owner named Olviero caught George and Teddy's act at the Condor. The promoter convinced Olviero to hire George and Teddy and the Condors to appear in his clubs in Italy. They offered a month-long contract to appear in clubs he owned on the Via Veneto in Rome and at the Marina de Massa resort in Tuscany. In May 1965, George and Teddy traveled to Italy. They began rehearsing their songs in Italian; "When in Rome, do as the Romans."

Their departure received lavish press in the *San Francisco Chronicle*, as it was not only unusual to reach out all the way to San Francisco for Italian entertainment, but they were black to boot! African Americans were rarely seen in Italy. But the Italians were crazy about soul music and couldn't wait to hear the American singers.

At their first performances, the Italian audience respectfully stayed in their seats, which was different from the raucous crowds George and Teddy were used to back in the States. Song after song, the audience clapped and wriggled in their chairs, enjoying the show, but not getting up to dance.

Pete decided that he would change that. During a short break, Pete told George to get on the dance floor, sing, then grab the hand of a lady and lead her to the dance floor. He told them that it would be okay and probably the only way to enliven the crowd. That did it. Within a few minutes, the crowd packed the dance floor like fish spawning, doing the Twist, the Swim, Watusi, and every other dance. After that night, the audience knew just what to do.

"We were like gold," George later recalled. "All the Italian guys wanted to hang out with us because they hadn't seen or met any black guys over

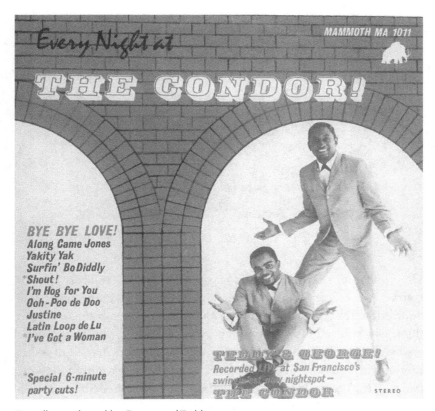

First album released by George and Teddy.

there, man. Pablo, the manager at Olviero's, told us that even the Italian men liked to hang out with us because we got all the attention."

Pablo also said that in those days Italian women often asked their doctors to tell their husbands that they needed sun and should spend some time at the beach. Their doctors would actually *prescribe* vacations on the beaches of the Italian Riviera! Olviero owned a second club at the beach of Marina di Massa, and George and Teddy also performed there.

Hamilton recalls that because of their dark skin, they would sometimes be asked, "Are you Sicilian?" to which they would reply, "Si, Sicilian."

The Beatles were appearing in Rome at the time, and contacted the manager of Olviero's Club 84, where George and Teddy were appearing.

The Beatles catch the George and Teddy show in Italy, 1965.

They told him they would like to see George and Teddy's act. "Of course!" was the reply, and the Fab Four were hustled in through a side door. All four of the Beatles got out on the dance floor to shake it up to the rock'n'roll sounds of the group. After the show, the Beatles were exuberant to meet George and Teddy and the Condors in their dressing room for drinks and photos. English bands were fervently following and copying the soul sounds originating from the United States. British singers Chad and Jeremy also came to one of their shows.

Gino joined Pete in Rome, with the agreement that he would take over managing George and Teddy and the Condors. Their North Beach friend Lucky Luccessi arrived with Gino and was ready for a party. Gino handed Pete $20,000 in U.S. dollars, his portion of the past month's profits. Pete was aghast! "What the hell do you want me to do with this? How do you think I'm supposed to get it back into the United States? I have to declare how much money I am bringing back in when we go home!"

Gino had never traveled outside of the United States and didn't know anything about the required customs declaration he would have to complete when returning. "I thought you'd be happy I brought it," Gino replied. "I'm sure you can figure out a way to spend most of it."

"Yeah, probably." Pete smiled.

Pete needed a haircut and found a suitable barbershop near the Via Veneto. Lucky Lucchesi tagged along. Pete was seated in the barber chair right away and a few men came in to wait their turn. Lucky was sitting in one of the chairs and decided he would pull one of his famous tricks on the group. He began messing up his long greasy hair and when no one was looking, he pulled his dentures out and turned them around inside his mouth. This created a huge gap in the front of his mouth with teeth protruding from each side of his lips. Suddenly he began to grunt. The barber looked at Lucky and figured it was just a normal body sound. Then Lucky grunted again, louder this time. Startled, the barber stopped cutting Pete's hair and wondered if Lucky was all right. After a minute or so, Lucky turned his face from the barber chair, then spun around towards the barber in a grunting roar with his mouth wide open, teeth gaping and eyes glaring! The barber dropped his scissors and ran to the back of the shop. One person flew out the door.

Pete had seen this trick before and was laughing hysterically. Lucky had done it again!

"It's a joke!" Pete yelled. "He's OK! He just wanted to scare you!"

Grinning, Lucky put his teeth back in place and rose, spreading his arms and exclaiming, "I just wanted to have a little fun."

Calm eventually resumed in the shop, enough for Pete to get a finished haircut, but he noticed the barber's scissors weren't quite as steady as before.

While in Rome, Teddy decided he wanted to drive a Vespa scooter. Though he had never driven a scooter, he thought it would be easy and it's what the Italians do, so he had to do it. Through their hosts, they rented a new baby blue Vespa, and George enthusiastically jumped on the back. Within minutes, Teddy had plunged through a huge plate glass showroom window in the City. George had seen what was coming and jumped off just in time to avoid injury. Teddy was also unharmed, but the Vespa and window weren't as fortunate. Pete picked up the tab for repairs.

Hamilton remembers, "Our flight had a stopover in Copenhagen, and we were contacted that they wanted us to perform at Tivoli Gardens. We were thrilled."

Before the show, a man asked Hamilton, "Are you Negro?"

"Oh, shit," George whispered, fearing that admittance to that fact could mean trouble. After realizing that it was an innocent question, George replied, "Oh, you, come on over here."

The women went crazy over George and Teddy. "A beautiful Danish blonde lady, having never seen a black man, asked if she could touch my face," George continued. "Of course, you can!"

"Teddy and I loved it. We were fussed over and treated with great respect in Italy and Denmark."

Back in the United States, George and Teddy recorded another album with Mammoth Records, *George and Teddy and the Condors – Just Like Me*, which would become their most successful record album. In 1966, the last single recorded with The Condors, *Nite People Make It/So I Cry* came out on Philips Records.

George and Teddy played at several venues after leaving the Condor, including Ciro's Le Disc in Hollywood, Tiger-A-Go-Go in the Hilton Inn on the San Francisco Peninsula, and Mr. Wonderful's in San Francisco. They appeared on KYA Radio's Surf Party at the San Francisco Cow Palace along with Little Stevie Wonder, The Beach Boys, Jan and Dean, Bobby Freeman, Dionne Warwick, and The Righteous Brothers.

In 1967, Condor saxophonist Jerry Martini paid a visit to Sylvester Stewart when he was working as a DJ on KSOL radio. Jerry told Sly that he had a great voice and he should just sing his entire show. Sly sang the weather, the news, the intros for all the songs, everything. Jerry told Sly that he thought they could form a great band. They hooked up to form a solid group, and Jerry played the saxophone with Sly and the Family Stone for years. He is the "Jerry" that Sly calls to in the song "Dance to the Music," when he sings, "Cynthia, Jerry. You might want to hear the horns blowin'." Jerry now performs with a tribute group called the Family Stone Band.

Sly Stone, Jerry Martini, and two other members of the original Sly and the Family Stone band, Cynthia Robinson and drummer Greg Errico, have been inducted into the Rock and Roll Hall of Fame in Cleveland.

Teddy Robinson passed away in 1985. George Hamilton lives in Scottsdale, Arizona, and still performs regularly at clubs and other venues.

10

Enter Carol

Sometime in January of 1963, Carol Doda was hired as a cocktail waitress at the Condor. Born on August 29, 1937, she was a 26-year-old, beautiful, sexy blonde with a perfect figure and lovely legs. Her breasts were normal sized for her thin body, which meant they were quite small. She was good at her cocktail job, flirty and willing to engage in conversation with anyone. (Her boyfriend at the time was John Burton, a recent law school graduate and bartender at Bimbo's who went on to become a California senator and U.S. congressman.)

The cocktail waitresses at the Condor wore leotards, pantyhose, and high heels. Most of the gals wore their hair ratted and coifed into an up-do or a straight cut style that reached the chin line. The "French Twist" was trendy as well. The beehive, a tightly ratted up-do pulled into a high swirl and sprayed to hold, was very popular. The girls who wore it were frequently teased as to what might be inside the beehive besides hair: spiders or mice?

Fat Davey developed a huge crush on Carol. He hung around her for hours and they established a deep friendship. They were two extroverts who loved life, laughter, and dance. They palled around, and Davey offered a little security for Carol when they walked the streets together.

Davey was constantly trying to lose weight. He didn't drink alcohol, but consumed several cans of diet soda a day. Carol favored white wine, and Davey looked after her at times when she had consumed a little too much.

Davey began urging Carol to dance on the bar when she wasn't busy serving cocktails. One night she took him up on his suggestion, jumping onto the bar and giving a lively demonstration of the Twist. The place went wild. Davey loved to dance too and would slide off the barstool and shake a leg on the floor.

Billy Dare, a popular gay entertainer who resembled Dean Martin, sang and played piano on Sunday nights and Carol would jam with him a bit. One night Billy suggested she jump up on the white baby grand piano and dance on top. He pulled the lid down to make a tiny dance floor. All she needed had been prompting. She kicked off her heels, and Billy assisted her onto his piano bench and up onto the piano. History was in the making.

"We were in the entertainment business with stiff competition; we were constantly trying to think of new gimmicks to attract business," Pete recalled. Dancing on a piano sounded novel and exciting at the time.

Carol began her piano-dancing career dressed in her cocktail outfit, which was a white leotard, black pantyhose or tights, and black high-heeled shoes. It began on Sunday nights with Billy Dare, but when Billy's show was over, she resumed serving cocktails, and danced whenever she could with other bands and entertainment.

Soon she was tagged as "Twisting Carol" or "The Girl on the Piano." Word got around town that she put on quite a show. Carol performed as "Twistin' Carol" at the Grodins Music Festival at the Oakland

The Twister

Twistin' Carol Dodo did a double-time twist to warm up for the Grodins Music Festival at the Oakland Auditorium on Sunday afternoon. She will appear with Dave Brubek, The Brothers Four, seven Playboy Playmates and other entertainers.

"Twisting Carol" dances in her cocktail outfit.

Auditorium on October 5, 1963. George and Teddy also performed that night, as well as The Brothers Four and The Four Freshmen. Adding to the exciting show were seven Playmates, "right out of the pages of *Playboy Magazine*."

Carol had been dancing atop the piano for a couple of months when Davey, sitting at the bar one night, was watching and thinking. George and Teddy were singing "Shout" with Carol doing the Twist on top of the piano. Suddenly, a crazy idea flashed into his creative mind. Why not raise the piano to the ceiling and have it descend with Carol on top and ascend back to the ceiling at the end of her performance? It was something that had never been done, and the Condor seemed like just the place to try it. He presented the proposal to Pete and Gino. Even though they had the lion's share of the street's entertainment business, they were ready to try any new trick to attract new customers.

"Yeah, what a gimmick!" Gino exclaimed.

"OK, let's look into it," Pete agreed.

Pete and Gino spoke to a few of their customers to find out if anyone knew of someone who could help with the piano idea. Almost everyone thought they had lost a screw and said it couldn't be done.

After reaching out to a few elevator companies in San Francisco, they became a little discouraged, thinking it would not be technologically possible. Finally, Pete called an elevator company in Oakland whose owner said, "Well, OK, I think I can do it. You'll need to gut the piano completely and make it as light as possible. Then maybe I can put it up there for you."

Pete and Gino knew nothing about pianos, but being determined do-it-yourselfers, decided to take on the job of removing all the inner workings of the baby grand. Pete says, "We banged on it with a sledge hammer, pried the strings with a crowbar, and pounded on it with hammers." Nothing budged. They were unable to remove a single part of the inner workings. "We didn't know what the hell we were doing," Pete recalls.

In desperation, Pete called a piano expert, who came to the club to help them out. After examining the piano and noting all the dents and scratches, he asked them what was going on. Pete told him what they had been doing to get the insides out, and the piano tuner asked if they had actually been banging on the harp.

"Well, yeah," Pete replied.

The piano guy screamed, "What? Are you guys nuts? There's enough tension in those wires to lift a cable car. One snapped string could take your head off!"

Pete and Gino turned white. The experienced piano man grabbed a screwdriver and proceeded to unscrew all the strings that were holding the harp in place. Then he carefully lifted the harp out. A very simple solution, but since the Condor owners didn't know a thing about pianos, they hadn't thought of using a screwdriver. They were very lucky nobody was injured trying to get the harp out.

After the harp was removed, Pete contacted the elevator guy in Oakland. He came over the club and attached the piano to four quarter-inch cables. The four cables were wound around a big shaft located in the attic area above the ceiling. The cables were placed two in front and two in the back next to the wall. The cables had to be wrapped tightly and evenly, resulting in equal pressure for each cable. It was tricky to keep the piano balanced, as it would tilt if the cable overlapped on the shaft or came off the tracks.

An opening was cut out in the ceiling above the piano. A long narrow tunnel was constructed from the girls' upstairs dressing room over to the hole in the ceiling. A person had to bend over to walk through it. Velvet draping was installed over the hole, which disguised it from view. There was a toggle switch located at the top, and one at the bottom. When flipped, the switch started the motor, which brought the piano either up or down. The dancers would simply step through the hole onto the top of piano, flip the switch, and the piano would descend quietly.

Pole dancing was unheard of at the time, and Carol had nothing to grab onto for balance so would sometimes clutch the elevator cables to steady herself during her dancing routines. If the piano tilted, it added a bit of comedy to her act, as the audience laughed and pointed while she desperately tried to hang on and not slide off the piano as it returned to the top.

The piano had to be in the down position to realign the cables, but straightening the cables had to be done from the top. Pete was usually the chosen one to go up, crawl through the tunnel in the ceiling, and adjust the cables. Typically wearing his expensive suit and tie, this was a dirty job he deplored. Sometimes he returned with black grease stains all over his clothing. Gino refused to do any of the dirty jobs, so whenever repairs were needed, Pete had to go fix it.

Merla Zellerbach wrote in her June 10, 1964, *San Francisco Chronicle* column titled "Here's a Piano with Sexy Legs":

"They done it wrong," cried Gino, North Beach's Cecil B. DeMille, "they sent her up too quick!"

He was directing a brave new enterprise, San Francisco's wildest nightclub gimmick—the girl on the airborne piano.

It all happened at the Condor, Broadway and Columbus, around 10 o'clock Friday night. A group of musicians, the Marketts, were stomping about the stage singing, "Girls are frisky in old Fris-co..." when somebody said, "That's a great song, Gino. Did they write it?"

"Whaddya think, I'm smart or sumpin'?" he answered, knocking over a table of drinks and lighting his 42nd cigarette.

His nerves, however, weren't the only taut ones. To the left of the stage, a tall bass player kept rolling his eyes heavenward. Directly overhead, suspended in air, hung a large white piano.

Suddenly the house darkened, the bass player raced for a corner, Twist music ground out loud and sensuous, and the huge instrument started its descent.

A canopy opened out of the ceiling and a pair of black mesh legs writhed atop the piano. Down, down it dropped, a torso appeared, centrally spotlighted, a mass of blonde locks, and finally, a face that brought a cheer from the audience.

It was Carol, the Twisting Cocktail Waitress! She bumped, wriggled, and rocked through a fast song, then the piano wafted gently upwards and its passenger disappeared through a hole in the ceiling.

"Does it stop automatically?" called a voice.

"Nah," said Gino, "it sails right on up to the sky . . ."

Despite his frustrated feeling that the act was too short, Gino was able to shout directions. "The wheels gotta come off and the piano's gotta drop lower so her head don't bump the ceiling!"

Then he turned to his friends. "Ya ever tried to gut a piano? You shoulda seen us yanking and tugging and trying to get the insides outta that thing. We finally called the piano man. He almost flipped when he saw what we'd done. 'YOU CRAZY NUTS!' he screamed, 'that piano's got a springboard with 140,000 pounds of pressure. It coulda knocked you right through the roof!' But that don't matter. This is gonna be a landmark that'll outlast us all."

"Gino, baby," said a pal, "you outta your lump? You wanna be remembered for THAT?"

"Yeah," he grinned, "Bimbo's got the girl in the fishbowl, and I got the girl on the piano!"

And whoever dreams up a way to put the fishbowl on the piano will REALLY have an act.

Several other performers were hired for the piano routine, but none were as popular as Carol. She eventually perfected her dance moves on the piano and became a master of dance seduction. She normally wore a white long-sleeved leotard, black pantyhose, and spiked high heels for her dance routines. Not topless, not yet.

Pete and Gino had tough competition, as the Broadway Strip had quickly become the entertainment center of San Francisco. A proliferation of new gimmicks was being introduced as club owners tried to come up with new ideas to entice people into their venues.

Judy Mac, wearing a fringed dress, strutted onto the stage at The Galaxie early in 1964, took a simulated plunge, and began to swim. Hence began a historic wave of dance moves that engulfed the nation.

Since the ceiling in the Off Broadway didn't have a space above, owner Voss Boreta couldn't have any contraption going up and down from the ceiling, although he had thought of it. He came up with the erotic idea of a bikini-clad woman dancing in a shower—a real glass shower with real running water. Swimmer Dee Dee, a voluptuously constructed young beauty with a gorgeous body, was Voss's star.

The Peppermint Tree up the street was doing SRO business as a dance club by letting the audience provide the floorshow. The large dance floor was elevated and specially lighted, allowing the dancers to see and be

A pre-silicone Carol dances "The Swim" in a real swimsuit; George and Teddy at right.

seen. Live rock'n'roll bands were booked regularly, including George and Teddy, who entertained there when not performing at the Condor. They packed the club.

Pete and Gino, the "kids on the corner" were stuffing wads of money into their pockets. Gino bought another brand new red Cadillac convertible, and Pete bought a white 1964 Kaiser Darrin, a fiberglass roadster convertible with doors that slid forward on tracks into the front fender wells of the car. The car demanded a lot of attention. Pete had a plaque made and installed it on the back of the car that read: MATTIOLI SPECIAL.

11

NIGHT ONE:
Topless Begins

"**B**ARE SWIMSUIT ARRIVES IN S.F**"** screamed the headlines above the *San Francisco Chronicle* masthead of the June 16, 1964, edition. "THE 'NUDE' SWIMSUIT" headlined the story on page 4, which told of the swimsuit's debut at Nasimo's, a small boutique in North Beach, the first to sell the suit. The first photos showed the model standing on the beach with the Golden Gate Bridge in the background. They were censored with banners across the bosoms of the model, but clearly showed the suit with woolen knit trunks and two thin straps of the same color and fabric joined together at the front, reaching up and over the shoulders, and attaching at the back of the trunks.

Nasimo Sargis proudly displayed a sign inside her shop that read, "WE RESERVE THE RIGHT TO REFUSE SERVICE TO WOMEN WITH STAGNANT FASHION IDEAS." This monokini was anything but stagnant. There was no bra, just the straps on top. Miss Sargis said that she felt that it was just a novelty for now, but in a few years, it would be the fashion. "Remember the furor when you first saw the bikini in America? Now you see them everywhere," she stated. She thought the suit would be worn for sunbathing, at home, or at private parties.

The fully endowed model stated that the suit was "comfortable and quite wonderful in its own way," but indicated that she would prefer to wear it in private.

Rudy Gernreich, an Austrian-born American designer and gay activist, had designed the suit. Miss Sargis carried a full line of Gernreich-designed clothing, and thus was able to be the first in San Francisco to offer his suit for sale. It came in a variety of colors and cost $26. The suit was available for purchase in New York as well, but some stores did not promote or display it. You had to ask for it. However, B. Altman & Company, Lord and Taylor, and Henri Bendel prominently displayed it for sale.

The following day, the *Chronicle* headlines blared: "INDIGNATION IN S. F. – BARE SUIT OUTCRY!" Once again, the headlines were at the top of the page, above the masthead. Featured prominently on the front page was a photo of one Sunny Adrey, at the age of four years, wearing a child's version of the topless bathing suit, two straps stretching over the shoulders and attached at the waist to the bottom part of the bathing suit. A second photo showed that same Sunny Adrey, now a saleslady at Joseph Magnin's Department Store, introducing the new version of the topless suit to a young adult woman. She had shared the photo of her as a child to prove that the topless suit was nothing new. The story continued:

> The local clergy were outraged. "Just two straps closer to moral decay," declared the Reverend Jacob Belling of Oakland's Neighborhood Church.
>
> "This is almost perversion," stated the Reverend Marlyn Anderson of the Nazarene Church.
>
> "It's probably designed to be provocative," said the Reverend James Roamer of Lincoln Park Baptist Church, "and in this sense might pose a threat to the public morals. But nudity apart from lustful purpose is not sinful."
>
> "Nakedness and paganism go hand in hand," warned Dr. Cecil J. Lowry of the Oakland Revival Tabernacle.
>
> Assistant Police Chief Alfred Arnaud stated, "Wearing the suit is a touchy, legal subject. Nudity isn't illegal unless it's lewd. This will have to be settled when they show up on the

beaches—and I guess they will. There are enough screwball women around."

Captain Daniel W. Kiely of Taraval Station, responsible for policing a long stretch of City beaches, observed that if a girl shows up in a topless suit "the main police problem will be the riot that occurs. The size of the riot probably will depend on how well she's endowed."

There was no suggestion that the suits would be banned from public beaches, but they'll not be allowed at City pools. "We don't even allow skimpy bikinis," said Martin Greenlaw, aquatic supervisor.

"My goodness!" exclaimed Alice C. Collins of Fleishhacker Pool. "It's chilly enough in a FULL bathing suit!"

Meanwhile, the suits were flying off the shelves. Miss Sargis sold her first order within a few hours of the photos appearing in the newspaper. She backordered another 14 suits, mostly for men, who said the suit was for their wives. At least that's what they said.

Herb Caen reported, "At Amelio's, Bill the Bartender asked Publicist Mike Watson: 'You gonna let your wife wear one of those topless bathing suits?' Mike: 'You think I want EVERYBODY to know I married her for her money?'"

Davey Rosenberg thundered into the Condor holding up a copy of the *San Francisco Chronicle* introducing the new topless suit.

"Look at this!" he said as he shoved the paper in front of Pete and Gino, who were sitting at the bar.

Pete stared at the suit muttering, "Wow! What next?" The paper was passed around to those at the bar bringing laughs, snickers, and lewd comments.

"We should put Carol in that bathing suit to dance on Billy's piano!" Davey exclaimed.

"What? Do you want to close us down?" Pete said. He thought the idea was just plain crazy. He just knew they would never get away with Carol

wearing that suit. Gino loved the idea, but was also skeptical they could pull it off.

That night when Carol arrived for work, Davey, Gino and Pete were waiting to show her the newspaper ad.

"Wow, do you think I should wear that?" she asked.

"Yes, you gotta do it!" exclaimed Davey. "You're a natural."

Carol stared at the photo of the model wearing the suit.

"Carol," said Gino. "You gotta do this!"

Carol smiled at the guys, thought for a minute, and then answered, "OK, I'll do it."

Davey raced down to Nasimo's and purchased one of the last swim-suits. When he returned with the suit, Pete and Gino held it up and inspected the top straps.

"Holy shit!" Gino exclaimed. "Not much to it!"

"I think I should call the cops and see what they think," Pete told Davey. Although Pete and Gino had a good rapport with the cops on the North Beach beat, Pete thought they would nix this idea immediately.

He was surprised when he called Captain Charlie Barka from the San Francisco Police Department to ask what he thought about the idea. Captain Barka's answer was very logical. "Well, we'll have to come and take a look."

"Yeah, I'll bet you want to take a look," Pete joked with Captain Barka. "You'd better come down."

He also placed a call to William Lockyer, Sr., father of one-time California Attorney General Bill Lockyer, who headed up the Alcoholic Beverage Control (ABC) Department at the state capital in Sacramento. He basically told Pete the same thing: "We'll just have to come and see what it is." They loved this part of their jobs.

Davey called Jim Lange, DJ at KSFO Radio, and several other movers and shakers to let them know about Carol's new outfit and drum up busi-ness. The news went out like a wildfire.

It was June 19, 1964. The Condor filled early in the evening and lines began to form down the block. Carol was upstairs in the ladies bathroom checking her black pantyhose for runs, dabbling with her makeup, and checking her ratted hairdo. She was very nervous, but excited and determined to do this. After all, topless photos had been featured in *Playboy Magazine* for years and Las Vegas shows featured topless dancers, so why not in San Francisco and why not her?

The club was packed, standing room only, with Pete helping out at the bar to fill drink orders being shouted at him. Gino greeted people at the door and tried to find them a place to sit. Newspaper reporters, along with radio and TV personalities, flashed their credentials. The papers were going crazy covering the story.

Finally, it was 9 o'clock. The Condor band began to play a rock'n'roll tune, and the piano began its descent. Carol was lying on her side with one leg cocked, wearing a flirty black lace cover over the topless suit. Wild cheering filled the room, as well as whistles, hoots, and hollers. The anticipation was overwhelming for some in the audience. They knew they were experiencing history in the making.

Slowly, Carol rose to her feet and began a gyrating dance. She began to fiddle with her little cover top as she turned around time and time again. Finally, she removed the cover and threw it onto the piano revealing the two-strap "topless" swimsuit. She didn't have much to cover, as her small, pert boobs peeked out from the sides of the straps. Audible gasps were heard from some members of the audience.

She danced the Twist and the Swim, thoroughly enjoying the enthusiastic reaction from her audience. Smiling, pouting, winking throughout the dances, she had the spectators in her hands. She teased the audience by placing the straps on and off her breasts, as if playing a peek-a-boo game.

Pandemonium filled the room, with the audience screaming, clapping, and stomping their approval. Pete, Gino, and Davey Rosenberg sat at the bar, flashing big smiles at each other and clinking their drinks. This was it! They knew they had a winner and were about to change the course of nightclub entertainment forever.

The audience wanted more. But, up went the piano with Carol still gyrating on it. If you wanted to see her again, you had to order another round of drinks at a two-drink minimum. "Another round!" was the call at most of the tables as they waited eagerly for the next show.

Carol wearing the first topless suit.

"Isn't that beautiful," exclaimed Gino. "A few weeks ago, she was a cocktail waitress and now she's a movie star!"

The next night, lines of excited partygoers were twice as long at the Condor entrance, with near riots at the door as people pushed and shoved to get in. Pete and Gino were trying their best to help the newly hired doorman and waitresses seat people and hold the number in the club to their allowed fire code numbers. They were having trouble accommodating friends and celebrities who showed up expecting special treatment. Each night that week was chaos at the door and inside the club.

Herb Caen wrote in his June 22, 1964 column:

I tellya this topless swimsuit thing is getting out of hand—or should that be phrased more delicately? Last Thursday night, Carol, the Swim dancer at Gino Del Prete's Condor, did her act sans bra, and the joint was immediately jammed to the rafters. Voss Boreta's rival Off Broadway got wind of these developments, whereupon his "Champagne" dancer, Dee Dee, shed the top of her bikini for her next show—and then HIS joint was jammed. North Beach is fast becoming Mammary Lane, and I have a feeling the next words you hear will be uddered by Police Chief Tom Cahill.

William Drury, reporter for the *San Francisco News-Call Bulletin*, wrote of his interview with Carol Doda, which appeared in the June 23, 1964 issue:

When Carol Doda, a shapely young blonde entertainer, makes her appearance at the Condor, she descends from above. Though not exactly like an angel.

She is lowered through a hole in the ceiling. On a piano.

On this piano, she does the Swim. Well, anyway, she wiggles. Purists may argue that Miss Doda does not really do the Swim, since that dance is essentially for couples, whereas Miss Doda wiggles alone.

The point is, she does it in a topless swimsuit.

The other night, in a desperate effort to keep abreast of the times, this column interviewed Miss Doda in her undressing-room.

The room was as starkly furnished as Miss Doda. Just an old couch, a chair, a table with a mirror, and a row of lockers. The only picture was a pornographic sketch scrawled on one of the lockers, which Miss Doda did not seem to notice.

She apologized profusely for a power failure during her act, which kept most of her audience in the dark about her talents.

Two narrow straps, crossed in front, provided inadequate covering for those talents.

Although she was not altogether in the altogether, enough of her was displayed to confirm the truth of the old saying that it is what's up front that counts. And one did not need to be much of a mathematician to count what was up front.

Being a shy, bashful lad, I did not quite know where to look.

"Do you have any hobbies?" I asked Miss Doda, gazing hard at the floor.

It was the sort of question a tongue-tied teenage reporter for a high school newspaper might ask his favorite movie star. That's how titillated I was.

"Good food," said Miss Doda. "Eating good food is my hobby. I like good food."

I examined the ceiling intently.

"Would you wear one of those swimsuits on the beach?"

"No," she said demurely. "After all, dancing like this is my job. I am paid to do it, I mean. I wouldn't want to spread it around thin."

I stared at the lockers, saw the pencil sketch, and hastily looked away. The room was getting warmer.

"Miss Doda," I creaked, "I have a very important question to ask you."

"Yes?" she said primly.

"How the heck do I get out of here?"

If necessary, I was willing to descend through that hole to the club below. With or without the piano.

I will say this for Miss Doda. In behalf of her employers at the Condor, Mr. Gino Del Prete and Mr. Pete Mattioli, she was determined to put up a good front—or bust.

The topless topic entered California governor Edmond G. Brown's weekly news conference when he was asked if he would serve as a judge in a controversial essay contest.

"I'd be happy to," he said, "but I wouldn't want to judge babies or a beauty contest."

"Even if they wore a one-piece bathing suit?" a reporter asked.

"I don't like those either," said the Governor. "I guess I'm just old-fashioned. I hope the women retreat from that very much."

There was a moment's silence before the Governor waved his hand. "Don't misunderstand me, gentlemen—I like women very much!"

Mayor John F. Shelley made a pointed reference to the fad at his news session, and indicated this was something City Hall can't fight.

He had conferred, the mayor said, with both District Attorney Thomas Lynch and Police Chief Thomas Cahill in the matter of a cover-up. Lynch reported that there was no law, to his knowledge, to cover this situation, and that the statute on indecent exposure applies almost exclusively to men. Cahill reported that he had studied the situation intensively and had reached the conclusion that the police had better "leave 'em alone, unless they become a police problem."

Police problem? "Well, if they create a disturbance, or snarl up traffic, or cause fights or rioting—well, then, they're a police problem," the chief said. He further explained that the girls could model the bare-bosom outfits and not become a police problem if they do so inside. "Unless," he added, "if it's a lewd show."

Mayor Shelley summed up: "I think too much is being made of a silly situation. Perhaps if we just leave it alone, the issue will go flat."

A few nights later, Mr. William Lockyer from the ABC and San Francisco Police Captain Charles Barka arrived at the Condor Club. After the initial cordial greetings, Pete offered them drinks, but they declined. They waited for Carol's performance and then watched attentively as she gyrated on the piano wearing the new "topless" bathing suit. They soon began to squirm as the straps intended to cover the nipples slipped and displayed, well, the nipples! Perky pink nipples popped out from a nearly flat chest and freely displayed their total nakedness.

After coming to their senses, the officials discussed the dilemma. They concluded that it might be all right for her to dance in that bathing suit as long as those nipples remained where they belonged: covered up by the straps. They told Pete that she would need to tape the straps over her nipples during her performance and that the nipples were never to be uncovered.

Pete instructed Carol to tape the straps to her body when she danced. She tried her best to tape them. However, in future performances, the straps remained in place for a while, but it wasn't long before her dance moves and perspiration caused the tape to release the straps from her body, revealing the total breast and yes, nipples. Dancing the Twist released the straps nearly every time.

Everyone in the City was talking about Carol's bathing suit that was supposed to cover the nipples, but didn't. Stern warnings came from Captain Barka's police force. Pete and Gino had a notion that it was only a matter of time before they would be busted for violation of the city's civil codes outlawing nudity. But for now, the cash registers were filling fast, and they weren't about to change anything unless forced to do so.

Carol's show was, in a way, a little nerve-wracking, as she spent lots of time trying to keep those itty-bitty straps over her itty-bitties. Her efforts became part of the show, but she knew that she had to attempt keeping the straps in place to show any undercover police that she was trying.

The clubs on and off Broadway were furiously competing for entertainment dollars, and soon many were featuring topless entertainment as well as or along with musical groups and singers.

The Condor continued to employ George and Teddy and the Condors and feature go-go girls, but the revolution was happening and the go-go girls began dancing topless as well.

The Condor operators were not the only club owners on the street who were worried about getting busted. A couple of weeks later, Voss Boreta introduced topless dancing in his club, the Off Broadway, across the street from the Condor. The Off Broadway seated twice as many people as the Condor and was now offering topless dancing in a much bigger venue with a large stage and theater-like seating. Voss had built a shower stall into the wall, a real glass shower with running water. His first topless dancer was Dee Dee, "The Girl in the Champagne Shower." Dee Dee was a voluptuously constructed brunette with a wide smile who was less enthusiastic about topless than Miss Doda was. But, as her boss put it, "Well, you know, she has, uh, well . . . more."

Voss was dating Yvonne d'Angers, an Iranian immigrant, who soon became his star attraction. Yvonne, who eventually married Voss, was a beautiful blonde with a flawless figure, Voss nicknamed his girl-friend "The Persian Lamb," and she quickly became Carol's primary competition.

There was a pseudo-friendly rivalry between the club owners, and they frequented each other's clubs often. They met for lunches and dinners at New Joe's, Vanessi's, or Swiss Louis and, over a meal or drinks, would try to figure out what the other club owners were up to. They all wanted to stay on top of the latest music and dances, and hire the prettiest girls.

One night in 1964, the league-leading Philadelphia Phillies dropped in, according to an item in Herb Caen. But the coach shouted "Midnight curfew!" shortly before Carol was due to descend from the ceiling. "Just a few more minutes," begged the players. "Nope," yelled the coach. "You're out of here!" Loud grumbles were heard from the crowd as several men reluctantly downed their drinks and rose to leave the club.

One month after the Condor "went topless," the club was fined for serving a minor, under age 21. It was a sting set up by the Alcoholic Beverage Control office in the City. A mature-looking teen was commissioned to fake his age, thereby gaining access to the club. A twenty day suspension of serving alcohol was levied against the Condor, but ten days of that were waived to "assure future compliance" with regulations of the ABC. Pete and Gino figured that the bust was a veiled warning and harassment for continuing their topless entertainment.

Over at the Sinaloa Club, Gino's wife, Gloria, decided she needed to jazz up her act a bit to compete with the topless entertainment popping up around the neighborhood. She commissioned furrier Gene Brunelli to fashion up a $360 chinchilla bikini for her to dance in. The new attire received widespread press but wasn't very durable and she later turned it into a chinchilla hat.

Pete and Gino decided to commission the manufacture of an ermine swimsuit bottom for Carol. Costing $1,000, the suit was silky soft and sexy, made from the luxuriously exquisite fur of ermine, a slim little creature belonging to the weasel family. The suit required refrigeration, and soon fell apart.

Various designs of the "topless" swimsuit were suddenly available in stores and quickly made their debut on the Swim- and Twist-ing dancers in North Beach. Carol wore several styles of the bathing suit, including a black leather suit and a checkered knit version. But the one thing they all had is common was a fully covered bottom and two straps above the waist.

Judy Mac, already famous for doing the ultimate Swim dance at The Galaxie, explained her topless act this way: "There are only three things to remember in the Swim. Move your arms in some sort of swimming motion—backstroke, crawl, or breaststroke—don't touch your partner, and you must wear underpants. After that, anything goes."

Big Al's retaliated the new competition with Tosha, the 74-pound "Japanese Doll" who stated that due to her Catholic upbringing, she was very embarrassed by "all this." To mollify her feelings, Big Al had the room darkened and fluorescent lights installed to illuminate her skimpy costume, leaving a little to the imagination. She was billed as "The Glow Girl."

The El Cid, Pierre's Tipsy's, and The Beach quickly dove in with topless Swim acts. The Playboy Club Bunny Room advertised their swim dancers with this ad: "SEE THE TWISTING BUNNIES SWIM." The SPCA stated their opposition to the ad, but their objections went nowhere.

By November 1964, several entertainment venues outside North Beach were experimenting with topless entertainment. The only club at San Francisco's Wharf, the Chart Room, was featuring a topless swim dancer. The Moulin Rouge was featuring Amateur Striptease contests. The Robinhood, San Francisco's newest nightclub presented "musical attractions the Chicagoans, direct from the Copacabana in New York, with gorgeous dance girls and swim dancer, Janet Raye."

Even artists sketching nude women posing inside the clubs became a thing. The owners of Mr. Wonderful decided that it would be much more cost-effective to hire a nude model and one artist than to pay for dancers and musicians. They hired model "Judette the Nudette" and artist Robert McClay to paint her while the tune "March of the Gladiators" played from a phonograph. This novel approach to entertainment was short lived, quickly losing its artistic value, excitement, and profitability.

Other entertainment competition around town that year included a teenaged Wayne Newton appearing in the Fairmont's Venetian Room and Vince Guaraldi at the El Matador. Yet nothing was even remotely as exciting as the topless clubs in North Beach.

Tourists began to include the Condor on their "must see" list while visiting San Francisco. While in Las Vegas, most tourists were comfortable taking in certain strip and burlesque clubs or cabaret entertainment such as the Folies Bergère. In 1957, Minsky's Follies at the Dunes Resort had become the first in the nation to debut topless showgirls on the Las Vegas strip—and packed 'em in. Aunt Betty and Uncle Henry from Omaha would never consider going to one of these types of show back home, but after a few cocktails and wine with dinner, everything changed. Over time, this attitude spilled over into San Francisco, and at a mere suggestion, tourists would pour into topless North Beach clubs for some after-dinner excitement. Some of the nation's most well-known celebrities were regulars, and thousands of locals considered it a must to visit to North Beach either for dinner or after-dinner cocktails and entertainment. Well-dressed couples, college groups, political heavyweights, and regular folks celebrating an anniversary or birthday made the stop at the Condor or other topless clubs in the area.

Pete answered a call one night and quickly recognized the voice at the other end of the line.

"Hello. This is Walter Cronkite. Would it be possible for me to reserve that table in the corner tonight around 10 p.m.?"

"Sure, I think I know which one—the one with the small partition in front of it?" Pete asked.

"Yes, that's it," was Walter's reply.

"How many will be with you?" Pete asked.

"Six," Walter said.

"Alright, it will be ready for you." Pete replied.

When in town, Walter Cronkite, known as the "most trusted man in news broadcasting," called Pete on a regular basis to reserve the secluded table in the corner. Since he would otherwise be easily recognized, he and his friends knew they could enjoy a little privacy there.

"Frank Sinatra is outside, Pete!" screamed the Condor barker another night. "What, you gotta' be kidding!" Pete exclaimed. He went outside, walked down the waiting line, and found Frank with a small group of people. "Come with me," he said. Frank and his entourage followed him back into the Condor and were seated in the VIP section for the show.

Clint Eastwood, Walter and Margaret Keane, Sal Mineo, Lenny Bruce, Sammy Davis, Jr., Joe DiMaggio, Rocky Marciano, Steve McQueen, Buddy Greco, Bill Cosby, Jack Palance, Caesar Romero, and Tony Bennett were just a few of the celebrities who stopped by for the Condor experience.

Of course, many of the celebrity men were there to get laid. Often, Pete would buy them a drink and introduce them to a young lady. He left it up to them to score points with her.

Sometimes Pete would just disappear. "I'll be over at Tipsy's," he would tell his employees. "Call me there if you need me." He was careful not to give anyone the idea that he was actually pimping women to the star crowd. Also, he didn't want to put his female employees in the position of feeling obligated to entertain any men, but he did provide many "cordial introductions."

12

Twin Peaks

A few months after Carol bared it all in her topless début, Pete noticed that Carol's breasts were getting bigger. He decided to ask Gino about it the next day.

"Naw, you crazy? They're the same," Gino stated with confidence.

Gino already knew that Carol was receiving silicone breast injections, but had promised her he wouldn't tell anyone.

"Well, maybe I'm imagining it, but I really think they are," Pete replied, unaware that Gino already knew about it.

A couple more weeks passed, and Pete was even more convinced Carol's breasts were growing ever larger.

When he arrived at the Condor that evening, Pete said to Gino, "Hey, Gino. I think something is going on with Carol's tits. They're getting bigger!"

"Bullshit!" Gino shouted. "What makes you think that?"

"I looked at them last night! They're bigger!" Pete yelled. "You know, I think this is all bullshit! I'm going upstairs and find out what's going on."

He climbed the stairs and knocked on the dressing room door.

"Come in," Carol responded.

Carol approves of the results of her silicone injections.

Upon entering her dressing room, he saw Carol sitting on her vanity chair facing the mirror. Looking into the mirror, he could see huge black and blue marks on her breasts. She was applying warmed moistened washcloths to her breasts as compresses, placing them where she had received silicone injections. She was attempting to warm the silicone, softening it and shaping it to smooth out the lumps that resulted from the shots.

"Carol, what are you doing? Are you nuts? What are you doing to yourself?" Pete demanded.

As Carol slathered thick pancake makeup onto her breasts, she responded, "Leave me alone, Pete. It's my body, you know. Get off my back."

"Carol, this is crazy. You doing that silicone shit? You don't know where that stuff goes inside your body; what it's doing in there."

"I'll do what I want with my body, Pete. It's none of your business."

Pete stared at her as she continued applying the makeup.

"Fine. I think you're crazy, but if that's what you want to do," Pete said, shaking his head as he left the room.

In 1964, it was extremely difficult to find a doctor in the United States who was willing to inject silicone into the breast tissue of a human. Most reputable doctors rejected the idea outright and wouldn't think of doing it. However, other doctors were willing to wade into the dangerous swamp of risky medical practices.

An English chemist, Frederick Kipping, pioneered the study and development of silicon polymers, an organic compound based on the element silicon. He coined the phrase *silicone*, which came to be used in sealants, adhesives, lubricants, cookware, and insulation. Beginning in 1954, medical grade silicone had been used sparingly in plastic surgery applications to fill out soft tissue deformities. Some doctors acclaimed its qualities of durability and compatibility with human tissue, but it was still considered experimental by most of the legitimate medical world.

The *San Francisco Chronicle* reported that Japanese doctors had developed an injectable version of silicone that contained a "secret ingredient" thought to form scar tissue around the injection, keeping the substance in place. Dow Corning Corporation first introduced pure medical grade fluid silicone in the United States under rigid restrictions and control. In the early 1960s, it was only available to six physicians in the States, and none were practicing in the Bay Area. Those six doctors were forbidden to inject it into human breasts.

Two Bay Area physicians, Dr. Paul J. Schneider of Oakland and Dr. Mark Gorney of San Francisco, both members of the American Society of Plastic and Reconstructive Surgery, had done extensive investigations of fluid silicone injections. Dr. Schneider noted that a major and possibly dangerous mystery has often been seen after silicone injections: about 20 per cent or more of the silicone literally vanished from the area of the injection. It just disappears, apparently "migrating" elsewhere in the body. It can't be recovered from body wastes, and whether or not it can harm human body cells was the big unknown.

Neither Dr. Schneider nor Dr. Gorney was in favor of silicone breast injections. They had seen horribly discolored silicone-injected breasts and believed there was extreme danger in the practice. At that time, there was no evidence that the practice could cause cancer, but both knew that silicone injections in the breasts could completely hide the presence of small cancerous tumors in an X-ray or mammogram.

Dr. Schneider was quoted as saying, "This is playing with a patient's life—quite literally."

The doctors stated in their report that breasts injected with silicone could never be restored to their original state of normalcy. They concluded that it would take years to study the effects of silicone injections before the procedure could be considered safe. [This outdated practice has in the years since been replaced with several forms of breast augmentation, including sterile salt water and silicone gel implants, both of which are known to be benign.]

Since the FDA had not approved the procedure, it was illegal. However, several obliging quacks in San Francisco were available to inject the fluid silicone for a price, and several young women were willing to risk the unknown consequences. Most women who had undergone the injections were not keen to talk about it. The dancers of North Beach had a somewhat different view: they were willing to let their secret be known to the world.

David Perlman, science correspondent for the *S.F. Chronicle*, reported in 1965 that each week for several weeks the women would first receive a small injection of painkiller to alleviate any pain. After it had taken

Voss Boretta's star, Yvonne D'Angers, on stage at the Off Broadway.

effect, the silicone would be administered into the breast through a large needle. Each injection would contain around a half ounce of silicone, which was the consistency of mineral oil. The injections also could easily add a pound of weight to each breast, and with age, cause the breasts to sag lower and lower. A firm, youthful breast could eventually become a drooping, heavy bag full of oil.

Carol admitted that she was really scared when she first went to the doctor. She said that he sometimes injected near the surface of the skin, but most needles penetrated deep within the breast. She admitted that the injections were very painful, with sharp pain sometimes shooting down both arms. She experienced some soreness, which she said rapidly went away.

According to an interview conducted years later by Julian Gutherie, a staff writer for the *Chronicle* and published online in *SFGate*, Carol stated, "I'd never heard of it [silicone], but my boss said, 'There's this doctor who's enlarging breasts. Maybe you should check it out.' I went from a 36B to a 44D. I was full of silicone. The injections came from what looked like a horse needle. The audience liked the outcome. They'd come every week to see how much I'd grown."

Pete confessed that he could never figure out why bare breasts were such a big deal to so many people. "It's just tits," he would often say. "Everybody's got 'em. Some are just bigger than others." And Carol's were now definitely bigger than most.

As soon as word of Carol's "bigger than most" breasts got out, the lines again formed outside the club.

Capitalizing on the impressive size of Carol's boobs and the attention they received, several companies hired her to promote their products. Tie manufacturer Beall J. Ernst was dismayed by the lack of imagination in the way most ties were displayed and in most tie designs. He decided to market his striped ties by a new method: sealed inside a can. He hired Carol to display the ties by pulling them out of a can beside her abundant breasts in a photo op.

Liquor distributors tapped Carol to appear at their promotional functions. In June of 1965, Smirnoff introduced their new drink "The Smirnoff Mule" with Carol appearing live and dancing at the Northern California Liquor Distributors event. The Smirnoff Mule combined Smirnoff Vodka and Seven-Up and was touted as "A Swinging Drink!"

Chief Cahill wasn't happy with the goings on inside and outside the North Beach clubs. The topless acts were becoming more and more brazen, and some of the other powerful people in government thought things had run amuck in their beautiful city. Mayor Shelly had had enough and decided that it was time to put a top on the bare breasted performers. Some of the San Francisco Board of Supervisors agreed— with the exception of Supervisor George Moscone, who was a regular

SXP120302-12/6/65-SAN FRANCISCO: It comes in a six-pack so naturally bartender Pete Matioli serves it up to Condor topless star Carol Doda. The unique gift packaging was the brain-child of tie manufacturer Beall J. Ernst who got into the tie manufacturing business over ten years ago when he was dismayed at the lack of imagination displayed in most tie designs. He now markets his striped ties in this new method just in time for the Christmas shopper. UPI TELEPHOTO sh/sh

Pete admires Carol as she pulls ties from a can.

at the Condor. He loved the energy down on Broadway and considered it the center of life in the City. Pete and George, close friends, had been classmates at Galileo High School who liked to party together.

Pete and Gino knew the days were numbered as to when the cops would crack down on topless entertainment. Davey Rosenberg knew it too, but saw a totally different side of the issue. Davey used the threats of a crackdown for publicity purposes by telling people that they'd better see Carol Doda before the cops cover up her beautiful assets.

As another of his wacky publicity stunts, Davey Rosenberg talked Pete and Gino into insuring Carol's twin 44-inch breasts for $1 million. Lloyd's of London issued the insurance policy.

13

NIGHT TWO:
Busted!

Clint Mosher, in an article in the *San Francisco Chronicle* on Friday, April 23, 1965, put it this way:

GRINDING IT OUT—UNTIL...

The hour was 9:10 last night. North Beach was jumping with bump-and-grind dancers and the blaring of four and five piece combos.

But there was something wrong. You could sense it and like the windless, sultry air, which precedes an earthquake. You could see it on the faces of the owners of the swing joints.

Business was booming but their faces were as long as a person who senses he's going to get hit where it hurts most—the pocketbook.

And at 9:15 came the earthquake.

By April of 1965, the North Beach street scene was slowly becoming one of raucous youngsters, gaudy sleazebags, showbiz characters, and alcohol-fueled tourists, resulting in fistfights inside and outside the bars. Calls to the San Francisco Police Department skyrocketed as theft and other crime rates increased.

Pete, Gino and Carol leave the Condor and are driven to the San Francisco Police Department to be booked.

The local residential community decided they had had enough. They filed grievances with the San Francisco Supervisors and formed an action group called the Telegraph Hill Dwellers. They requested that more cops patrol the area, prompting Mayor John F. Shelley to call a public meeting on the crime situation. Chief of Police Thomas Cahill assigned extra patrolmen to keep order, and arrest or detain criminals. Although the residents insisted that they were not the morality police, it was well known that they simply didn't like what was going on down on Broadway. They insisted that they were just trying to protect their lives and property.

On April 22, it was reported in the *S.F. Examiner* that police action would soon be taken against the topless clubs and girlie shows due to violations of public decency, lewdness, and pornography.

Davey Rosenberg advertised the promised raids by boldly posting the police chief's threat in showcases outside the Condor. When Big Al Falgiano was at the Hotsy Totsy, before he opened his own Big Al's, he had staged a mock raid every night to close the show. Club owners were holding their breath, but the audiences were getting bored with the same old topless swim shows. They wanted a main attraction—a police raid.

That night, a small group of nicely dressed men and women dressed as tourists paid the door charge and walked into the Condor. Once inside, they asked to see Pete and Gino. The club owners were expecting something since the word was out that a showdown was imminent. Davey Rosenberg wanted it to happen sooner rather than later, as he knew it would bring an avalanche of publicity to the club.

They walked over to Gino and informed him that he was under arrest.

"You gotta' be jokin'," Gino replied. "You guys finally did it."

"Where's your partner?" the officers demanded.

"Over there," Gino answered, pointing to Pete sitting at a table.

They approached Pete, and demanded he get up. "You're under arrest."

"What for, man? What are the charges?"

"I think you already know," the Alcohol Beverage Control officer smirked. "Where's Carol?"

"She's upstairs," Pete replied.

Carol was in her dressing room getting ready for her performance when the cops ascended the stairs and knocked at the door.

Leaving Broadway after arrest. Pete center front seat, Carol center back seat, Gino on her left.

"San Francisco Police Department!" they shouted. "Open the door!"

Carol appeared frightened as she opened the door and was told she was under arrest.

"What for? I haven't done anything wrong!" screamed Carol.

"Indecent exposure. We're taking you to the station, so better grab a coat," the officer said. Shocked and angry, Carol complied.

Raids were simultaneously taking place at several other topless clubs along Broadway or Columbus in North Beach, resulting in the arrest of fifteen additional dancers and twelve more owners and managers including the owners of the Chi Chi and their seductive brunette star, Carol Jane Davis; blonde bombshell Baby Jane Dunn at Big Al's; and the owner of the Off Broadway, Voss Boreta, along with his beautiful "Persian Kitten" dancer, Yvonne D'Angers. In addition, there were arrests at the In-the-Round, Tipsy's, Moulin Rouge, and Mr. Wonderful. Five other clubs located the City were also raided during the span of the raids, which took 4½ hours.

The women quickly grabbed kimonos and coats to cover their skimpy attire and were shoved into waiting police cars. They protested to the police, to no avail.

A large crowd had gathered in the street, watching the spectacle. They began chanting, "We want girls! We want girls!"

One bystander declared, "We need Mario Savio." Mario Savio was a prominent leader of the newly formed Free Speech Movement at the University of California, Berkeley. Most in the crowd figured that topless dancing should be considered a form of free speech, and they supported it. Many in the crowd were either affiliated with a North Beach establishment or tourists excited to be a part of the action happening before their eyes.

All the owners and dancers were taken to police headquarters for booking.

Pete, Gino, and Carol were locked into the same holding cell while the paperwork was completed. As Carol's tears flowed, the police officers on the North Beach beat kept walking by them laughing, and jokingly asking them, "Hey, what are you guys doing here?"

Most of the officers knew that there was going to be a raid at some time, but they had made friends with the club owners and dancers. They knew Pete and Gino, and quite enjoyed the required club check while they were on duty. Many frequented the clubs while off duty as well.

The Condor crew was booked, fingerprinted, and released, all within an hour. Carol was charged with indecent exposure, disorderly conduct, and outraging public decency. Pete and Gino were charged with keeping a disorderly house. Those charges were pretty much the same for all other arrests that night at the affected clubs. Bail for the women was set at $770 and for the club owners at $1,100. Bail was met for all arrested. They were released, and most went back to their respective clubs for a drink.

Pete, Gino, and Carol returned to the Condor to raucous cheers from the bouncers, bartenders, and cocktail waitresses. Davey Rosenberg made sure the show went on with the band continuing to play. Dancers jumped back onstage, but now they were all wearing tops. One dancer at Big Al's took to the stage wearing stretch pants and a turtleneck sweater, simply to make a point.

Deputy Police Chief Al Nelder said it was the department's "first step in cleaning up the nightclub situation in North Beach." Nelder said that "arrests will continue as long as the violations continue, possibly right up to bar closing time at 2 a.m. today."

Jesuit-educated Mayor John F. Shelley was eager to make newspaper headlines and political points. He knew that timing of this sting had been critical. He made the announcement at a University of San Francisco alumni banquet he was attending at the Fairmont Hotel. "The cleanup of Broadway is beginning," he declared to the audience. According to the *San Francisco Chronicle*, he stated, "I've been waiting for some time to be able to make this announcement. As of nine o'clock tonight, certain 'invasions' are taking place along Broadway to inform those places that the Swim is all right—but only with a top."

In all, thirty-two San Francisco police officers and agents from the State Alcohol Beverage Control Department carried out the raids.

The headline of the April 23, 1965, edition of San Francisco's evening newspaper, *The News-Call Bulletin*, proclaimed, BROADWAY WILL FIGHT BACK.

"There's nothing obscene about my dances," insisted sultry brunette Carol Jane David, 30, of Club Chi Chi. "My dances are, oh, so wonderful. In one of them, my bridal number, I come on stage in a full-length veil. At the end of my number, I'm wearing a satin bikini and two rosebuds."

Baby Jane Dunn, 24, of Big Al's, also put on a good front. "I've been a showgirl for four years, and I've never done anything to be ashamed of. I wouldn't be embarrassed to have my parents see me dance."

Attorney Harry Wainwright declared, "We're not going to conform to the whims of the mayor or the censorship of Police Chief Thomas Cahill. The raids were just a grandstand show to terrorize the owners and the entertainers. They can't grind us down. We'll fight for this right to the Supreme Court, if necessary."

The next morning several fully covered dancers appeared at Municipal Court, waving to a crowd of more than a hundred onlookers. Many in the crowd waved back, but were simply there to see what a real live topless dancer looked like.

Judge Donald Constine delayed some charges until the next week, giving the arrested time to work on their case with their attorneys.

That night, lines began to form in front of the Condor and other clubs before opening time. North Beach was jammed with eager partygoers. San Francisco had come to support topless dancing as a form of entertainment inside a club where alcohol was served. The lines got longer with each passing night.

The Mayor was quick to respond declaring that having fun was part of the City's heritage, and that he was not against the people of San Francisco having fun. But he and the Chief of Police Cahill had been receiving criticism from that what was happening on Broadway was not only obscene, but illegal and he'd better do something about it.

Captain Charles Barca stated that he and Sargent Robert Davis, chief of the vice squad, would be making checks personally and that arrests would be made as long as violations continued. Well, of course they would be keeping *personal* tabs on the clubs.

During their performances, the dancers began to make trivial efforts to cover themselves in a way that might pass the glaring eyes of the undercover police. But their hearts were not into pleasing the cops. The dancers knew that the cat was out of the bag, so to speak, and that there was a big fight ahead. Uncertainty was in the air.

At her next performance, Carol Doda attempted to cover her bulging boobs with a thin gauzy fabric. She was aghast when a policeman jumped up onto the stage and told her to cover up. She slithered off the piano and burst into tears.

"Please stop crying," Gino pleaded.

"You haven't been arrested," cried Carol.

"But I have," Gino reminded her. "And so has Pete."

"Poor Carol Doda," quipped Herb Caen in his column. "Here she goes and spends all that money on silicone injections—to increase her bust measurement from 32 to 36—and now the cops have ordered her to cover up."

14

Topping
the Topless

S ix days after the bust, Pete called a meeting with several North
Beach club owners, the major players in the topless and nude entertainment industry. They decided to form an association to address
the complaints they were receiving from the police department, the ABC,
and City Hall. They called themselves the Broadway Businessmen's
Association.

At a meeting at the Fior d'Italia Restaurant, members of the association agreed that the San Francisco Fire and Police Departments were
harassing them. Inspectors were being sent to the clubs much more
frequently, citing the businesses for violations of regulations, some of
which the association members had never heard of before.

It was true that some establishments had never bothered to obtain the
necessary permits to operate in North Beach. There was an $8.00 permit
for "a place of public assembly" that several clubs had never acquired
from the Fire Department under a new mandatory code. Some were also
violating sanitation standards set up by the City's Health Department.

The association members agreed they would try to put a new face on
their businesses, one that was acceptable to the neighborhood popula-
tion. A supervisor and attorney for some of the clubs, George Moscone

(later to be mayor), spelled out new rules agreed to after negotiations with local groups and city officials.

Mayor Shelley announced the new rules at a news conference:

⊚ Nude or semi-nude females would not be allowed to work as waitresses.

⊚ No off-color or nude entertainment will take place where minors are allowed.

⊚ Only legitimate fashion shows are approved in establishments whose license is primarily for restaurant use. The clothing modeled must actually be for sale.

⊚ Doors and windows will be kept closed or covered so that any questionable entertainment cannot be seen from the street.

The Alcoholic Beverage Control Department stated that they would allow nudity if confined to the stage, and agreed to limit the number of new liquor licenses granted to new venues in the area.

Mayor Shelley and Police Chief Cahill jointly expressed their gratitude that the operators had seen fit to exercise some "voluntary control." "It means that much less grief for us," he said.

Cahill and Shelley both said they rated auto and pedestrian traffic as Broadway's major problem, as the shows attract huge crowds and the street served as the ingress and egress of the Embarcadero Freeway. No other type of traffic was mentioned.

As to the voluntary restraint now hovering over Broadway, there seemed to be some difference of opinion. As reported by the *San Francisco Examiner*, Police Captain Barca, commander of Central District, which includes the semi-nude area, said he had asked the operators to plaster pasties on their performers' breasts or cover them with net or mesh.

"I can't force them to do it," he said. "But I'm keeping my fingers crossed in hopes that they will."

"We are constrained by recently repealed vagrancy laws passed by the State Legislature, which restrict my men from cracking down on the 'undesirable element' that is attracted by nudity," Captain Barca explained. "But don't misunderstand me," he continued. "The shows attract the wealthy set too. They attract anybody who likes a little action now and then—and who doesn't?"

The Wednesday, April 28, 1965, edition of the *San Francisco Chronicle* had this to say:

The Broadway Businessmen's Association decided at a luncheon meeting "to go along the way we're going," according to Peter Mattioli, co-owner of the Condor and a member of the association's board of directors.

Which means topping the topless until a court ruling is handed down. But "it's hurting us," Mattioli commented sourly.

Beleaguered Mayor John F. Shelley also braved the North Beach area for lunch yesterday. He was the picture of the jolly politician, glad-handing everybody. Except Carol Doda.

Miss Doda, of the 40-inch statistic, used to do a topless dance atop a piano in the Condor, Columbus Avenue and Broadway. That ended Thursday night when a police officer arrested her, to the disgruntlement of customers and the proprietorship alike.

While the Mayor was upstairs at the Montclair Restaurant, 550 Green Street, yesterday, describing to the North Beach Lions's Club the burdens of public office, Miss Doda sat in the bar below with the Condor's press agent, Dave Rosenberg.

Rosenberg explained that they had no intention of crashing the luncheon, but that "we just want to try to talk to him."

"We don't want to run a corrupt town," Miss Doda interjected plaintively. "We just want to do our shows."

But informed of their presence, the Mayor reacted angrily.

"I just heard that there's an inclination on the part of some people . . . to use this meeting as a source of embarrassment to you and me," he told the Lions.

"Downstairs there is a topless dancer trying to get in. I resent it. I don't like it."

Thus when the Mayor departed. Surrounded by a buffer of hand-grabbers and his own aides, he swept by Miss Doda and Rosenberg on the sidewalk outside without so much as a glance.

Repeatedly, Miss Doda called from the rear of the mob. "Mayor Shelley, may I speak with you please," but her cries went unheeded.

Left in the lurch, but still petulantly optimistic, she plumped
into Rosenberg's car and swept off to Cathy's at 2047 Polk Street
to replenish her supply of topless bathing suits, depleted by the
confiscations of her Thursday night arresters.

❖ ❖ ❖

Club owners vow to fight for rights to topless entertainment performances.

Captain Barca also confirmed that the nightspot operators were forming an association for their mutual protection and to do some self-policing. He named a committee of three as those heading up the project: Pee Wee Ferrari of Tipsy's, Pete Mattioli of the Condor, and Frank Dinatale of the Roaring Twenties.

He told the newspapers that Mattioli originated the association movement, as well as another one about a year ago that had flopped. He said his most recent conversation with Mattioli went like this:

"Did Barca ask you to put pasties or something on the girls?"

"Ask?" Mattioli replied.

"Well, did you agree to do it?"

"We sure did."

"What if he told you to cover up everything?"

"We'd do that, too. You think we want to go out of business?" Mattioli stated. "If the police want the girls to wear sweaters, then sweaters they wear. We don't want trouble."

The cops always wanted to get paid off. They asked Pete for $300. Pete never gave them any money, but Gino would sometimes pay them out of his own pocket. Pete thought it made Gino feel like a hood, an image he liked.

Pete would tell the cops, "What am I paying you for? I'm not doing anything wrong. What are you gonna bust me for? And besides that, I am very good friends with your boss, Captain Barka. He loves to come in and see the shows. The cocktail girls make him feel important. Which he is!"

"Can you get the ABC to look the other way?" Pete asked one of the cops. "If you can do that, I'll give you $600. Until that day comes, don't bother me." Naturally, when the ABC representatives came in they received all the free drinks they wanted.

Davey Rosenberg was right and most club owners who were worried about getting busted were wrong. The clubs received unabated publicity. The performers entertained packed houses and the wait lines continued around the blocks. You couldn't get into the Condor or Big Al's with a shoehorn. Club owners beamed with joy as they listened to the cash registers playing their favorite tune.

Everyone wanted to be part of it, to say they'd been there, they'd seen Carol's boobs or one of the other performers, and they were hip for doing so. Broadway was the center of it all in San Francisco—and for the United States for that matter.

Pete relaxes inside the Condor.

15

The Trials

The skilled and flamboyant attorney Melvin Belli pressed the court for a quick trial date in order to receive top billing and the most publicity for the Off Broadway and his client, Voss Boreta. He stated to the court that any delay would bring economic hardship to the Off Broadway dancers, waitresses, and a nude model. He pleaded that there were more people affected at the Off Broadway than arrested at the Condor. The court agreed with his request, and an unprecedented court date of two weeks from the time of arrest to trial was granted.

A much younger and inexperienced crew-cut colleague in the practice of law, Harry Wainwright, represented the Condor. He was given a court date eight days after Boreta's, which was later moved up to the same time as the Off Broadway trial. But the seasoned Mr. Belli received the lion's share of publicity, and the Condor trial was more or less relegated to an "also ran" status, even though Carol Doda was quite famous by that time.

The public quickly referred to the hearings as the "Titty Trials."

Confusion reigned throughout the separate trials involving the different clubs. Defense attorneys Patrick Hallinan and Melvin Belli defended the Off Broadway club owner, Voss Boreta, Yvonne d'Angers, and other Off Broadway bare-bosomed workers in the courtroom of Judge Leo R. Friedman. The prosecutor was John O'Brien.

Assistant District Attorney Thomas Norman was assigned to prosecute the case against the Condor. In the courtroom of Judge Leland Lazarus, attorneys Harry Wainright and Ed Fleishell defended the Condor Club.

The question before the attorneys hired to represent the clubs was, how do you select a "jury of your peers" at a topless trial?

All the jurors were asked if they had heard of or read about the cases, and most admitted that they had. Choosing a fair and impartial jury for each trial was challenging at best.

Rob Robertson, the *San Francisco Chronicle* reporter who covered the trials, wrote in his May 5, 1965, column:

"Do, ah, uh, bare breasts offend you, per se?" defense attorney Patrick Hallinan asked a female panelist, every verbal and facial effort bent to make the necessary question sound matter-of-fact.

"Have you, uh, ever been in one of these clubs where, ah, nudity or semi-nudity is featured?" probed prosecutor John O'Brien softly.

The juror's reactions were varied, but for the most part, they were quite blasé.

"You, ah, don't feel that what these girls have been doing is illegal, do you?" Melvin Belli asked one juror, his glasses sitting low on his nose as his eyes met hers directly.

"Well, I don't know," the matronly woman replied as she shrugged her shoulders. "That's what I'm supposed to find out, am I not?"

The prosecution was careful to exclude from consideration all nicely dressed men, married or not. They excused rough-looking longshoremen and men under the age of 40.

Attorney Hallinan suggested, sarcastically, the prosecutor could use the "blue nose" test. Rub some special litmus paper on a jurors' nose, and if it turns blue, dismiss them.

The defense promptly released all panelists who were closely associated with law enforcement officers and any plump, middle-aged women dressed in knit suits and pillbox hats.

"Do you consider pasties more offensive than bare breasts?" Mr. Belli asked one prospective juror.

"Do you speak as an expert, Mr. Belli?" interjected the judge.

Worried that his wife might be in the courtroom, Mr. Belli swung around and hastily scanned the audience. Judge Friedman gave him a reprieve.

"It's alright, Mr. Belli, you don't have to incriminate yourself," the judge said with a chuckle.

The attorneys for the Off Broadway interviewed 52 potential jurors, ultimately agreeing to a panel of four women and eight men.

Once a jury was seated, the trial of The People vs. Voss Boreta and three of his bare-breasted entertainers began.

Prosecutor John O'Brien presented a series of photographs taken by police shortly after the raid on April 23 and asked that they be admitted into evidence. The photographs showed defendants Yvonne d'Angers, Euraine Heimberg, and Kay Star in their usual working attire, sans tops.

Defense attorney Patrick Hallinan quickly objected, jumping to his feet in protest that the photographs were "inflammatory and prejudicial," and therefore, inadmissible. He cited the recent California and United States Supreme Court rulings in the still controversial cases of Dorado and Escobido.

Melvin Belli cited his own personal objections to a couple of photos of a scantily clad Miss d'Angers walking away from the camera.

"Is this the same girl?" he asked mockingly. "I can't tell from the smile."

The Dorado and Escobido rulings were cited as argument that evidence that is collected after police procedure shifts from "investigatory to accusatory" is inadmissible. In other words, evidence used after the point at which police have decided that they have the guilty party and intends to arrest them. Since all the evidence collected for trial was obviously obtained after the raiding officers stormed into the Off Broadway with the prior intention of making an arrest, Mr. Belli argued, it could not be used as evidence against his clients.

Judge Friedman listened to the argument intently. Their point intrigued him. He turned to Captain Charles Barca, who led the Off Broadway raid on orders from his superior and was the day's only witness.

"Let me ask you this, Captain. What did you go there for?"

Captain Barca squirmed in his seat.

"Didn't you go there to make arrests?" the judge pressed.

"Yes," Barca replied. "If what I considered to be violations of the law continued."

Meanwhile, the case of The People vs. The Condor was being held on the second floor of the Hall of Justice where Defense Attorney Harry Wainwright was addressing the same issue. He pressed Judge Lazarus to bar admission of photographs of the voluptuous Miss Doda's piano-top gyrations because of Dorado and Escobido case precedents.

At first the judge declined to bar them, but when he learned that they had not been taken on the same night Miss Doda was arrested for "lewd and dissolute" conduct, he agreed that they could not be entered as evidence.

A discussion ensued as to whether "lewd and dissolute" means the same thing as "obscene." Mr. Wainwright insisted that they are the same and that the Supreme Court has ruled that proof of obscenity must meet the same tests as the proof of "hard-core pornography."

Judge Lazarus recessed the trial and told the crowd that the issue would be hashed out in chambers before court resumed.

The Condor jury, eight men and four women, was identical in makeup to the one seated for the Off Broadway trial.

From the *San Francisco Chronicle*, May 7, 1965:

TOPLESS TRIAL – A QUESTION OF BARENESS

Bob Robertson

Next day the Off Broadway trial got down to the "nitty-gritty." The question presented to the jury was just how much breast can a woman expose for such conduct to be considered "lewd and dissolute" according to the San Francisco Police Department?

Hallinan asked Yvonne d'Angers to rise and remove the flowing scarf she wore above her form-fitting baby blue knit suit.

Pete, Gino, Carol, and Harry Wainwright discuss strategy for their defense.

"Now," he asked Officer George Cathrell, one of the April 23 raiders of the Off Broadway, "do you consider that lewd and dissolute?"

Hallinan gestured in the general direction toward direction Miss d'Angers low cut neckline, which exposed her impressive physical attributes.

Witness Cathrell, a bearlike man with ruggedly handsome features, wriggled uncomfortably in his chair and murmured, "No. No, I wouldn't."

Protesters against arrests of club owners and dancers.

Defense attorney Hallinan questioned Officer Cathrell repeatedly on the subject of how much exposed breast the police department considered lewd. Cathrell had trouble answering the questions definitively, so Hallinan walked to the courtroom blackboard. There he drew the profile of a woman's upper body and then lightly shaded on a slim bikini top.

"Is this obscene?" he asked.

"No, it is not," Cathrell responded.

Hallinan erased the bikini top and pared it down both in width and circumference. He did this repeatedly decreasing the perimeter with each drawing and asking Officer Cathrell the same question as to lewdness. Each time he made the drawing smaller until it barely resembled a bathing suit. Each time he was asked, the officer responded, "No, that is not lewd."

Finally, Judge Friedman intervened sharply: "If the nipples of a woman were exposed, that was the basis of the arrest, was it not?"

"Yes, sir," Cathrell replied quietly, and the issue stood defined for the record.

Prosecutor John O'Brien once requested that photographs made by the Police Department during the raid of the Off Broadway be entered into evidence. But the judge stood by his decision not to allow them.

O'Brien eventually was successful in subpoenaing and getting into evidence photographs made at the same time by photographers from all three of San Francisco's major daily newspapers.

Mr. Hallinan and Mr. Belli never objected to the newspapermen's photographs because they showed their clients in a less harsh light and also showed more of the clientele and beautiful club interior, both of which even the police agreed were "decorous."

On the second floor of the courthouse, the prosecution for the City's second "topless" trial—against Carol Doda and the co-owners of the Condor—rested its case after presenting the four police officers who made that raid April 22.

Defense attorneys Edward Fleishell and Harry Wainwright promptly asked Judge Leland Lazarus to throw the case out of court or direct the jury to render a verdict of not guilty. The prosecution had failed utterly, they argued, to prove beyond doubt that Miss Doda's piano-top gyrations were obscene according to "the contemporary standards of the community at large."

Judge Lazarus suggested he "might" grant their request later, but said the case was too important to the community for him to do so without hearing more testimony.

Wainwright then called Novella O'Hara, the *Chronicle*'s "Question Man," whom he subpoenaed as an expert witness on the community's contemporary standards.

Judge Lazarus overrode prolonged prosecution objections and allowed her to testify. Her job, he suggested, should give her some insight into such matters.

O'Hara's answer to Wainwright's question—was Miss Doda's dance offensive to contemporary community standards?—was a terse, "No."

Miss Doda, a blonde of amazing proportions, was also called to describe her act. Asked about the music it was set to, she replied: "Well, we have rock'n' roll music, so I wouldn't be doing the 'Tennessee Waltz' or the ballet to it. I'd look like a nut."

On May 8, 1965, under the headline: "TOPLESS" ACQUITTED, Rob Robertson of the *San Francisco Chronicle* had this to say:

JUDGE ORDER TOPLESS VERDICTS OF NOT GUILTY

The sword of justice punctured the over-blown crusade against bare bosoms in North Beach yesterday. Municipal Judge Leo R. Friedman, citing Constitutional guarantees and legal precedents, bluntly ordered a verdict of not guilty for the four defendants from the Off Broadway. He stated that the prosecution had failed to prove that the bare-bosomed posing of Yvonne d'Angers and waitressing of Kay Star and Euraine Heimberg was obscene in the eyes of the community.

"The test is not what a couple of people feel," he said.

"The test is what the people of San Francisco feel. No police officer can substitute his personal feelings of what is right and wrong." He continued, "Lewd and dissolute conduct is the same as obscene conduct, which the Supreme Court has clearly ruled

Condor jury.

must be proved by such a consensus, including the young and the old, the religious and the irreligious, the educated and the uneducated."

He also ruled that the performance of the defendants "partook of a theatrical production," which has certain guarantees of protection by the State and Federal Constitutions.

"This is a free country," he stated. "I think we have a right to pick and choose what we want to read and see. No one's pulling anyone's arms to drag them into these places in North Beach."

He also suggested there is a wide difference between indecent exposure, which means exposure of the private parts of genitals "with salacious intent" and the mere exposure of a human breast.

"I don't consider the human body lewd or obscene of itself," he said.

When the courtroom audience exploded into applause at the end of Judge Friedman's exposition, he reacted with characteristic anger at any disruption of the dignity of his court and gaveled them into silence.

Carol proudly displays the front page of the S.F. Chronicle.

Judge Friedman's trial ended in midafternoon. Following the lunch recess, he and counsel conferred in chambers, Assistant DA John O'Brien for the prosecution, attorneys Melvin Belli and Patrick Hallinan for the defense.

"Here we go," Mr. Belli whispered to Mr. Hallinan, smiling.

Belli promptly moved for the advised verdict, arguing briefly the prosecution had failed to make a case. Prosecutor O'Brien held that lewdness was a question of fact for the jury to decide.

Then the judge said, "I am going to pass on this motion and explain my reasons. They are as follows:

"Whatever was going on in the Off Broadway, as shown by photos and movies, was 'in the nature of a theatrical production' and thus was protected by Constitutional guarantees of free speech and assembly."

"As to community standards (he had ruled out testimony offered by state witnesses), he held that this depended on what the people of the entire city feel, not what the people of a particular segment may want.

"What is right or wrong is a matter of law, and no policeman can substitute his personal opinion."

The judge said he had looked up the words and that "lewd," dissolute" and "obscene" all mean the same thing, "shameful, morbid sex."

Then he cited a number of High Court decisions on obscenity. He read one, dealing with a book, and told the jury he was substituting the word "acts" for "book" to serve his purposes. He held the test of obscenity was its effect and the type of audience it reached. It might, he said, have no effect on a sophisticated audience and that to be acted upon it must "offend the common conscience of the community."

He read another case, which held that "the law does not undertake to punish vulgarity or bad taste."

He told the jury they had heard the evidence, seen the movies, and that there was nothing in any of it that would shock anyone. "Nobody was pulling anybody's arm to drag into this place," he said.

Lewdness, he then declared, is not a matter of fact alone, but of Constitutional law as well, which meant that the court as well as the jury could decide the case.

The judge declared there was nothing offensive about the female breast, that no one took exception to the sight of a mother nursing a baby while riding a bus. On the other hand, he said, indecent exposure meant exposure of the genitals. "I advise you to return a verdict of not guilty," Judge Friedman instructed the jury. "You don't have to if you don't want to. But if you bring in a verdict of guilty, I have the power to set it aside, and will do so."

The jury retired for deliberations and returned 14 minutes later with an acquittal for all defendants.

After the jury returned its verdict, Hallinan took the floor to call the judge's interpretations "the finest piece of Constitutional reasoning he had ever seen in a lower court. It would do dignity and honor to a Douglas or Black."

The judge grinned wryly and retorted. "Why don't you tell that to President Johnson?"

Minutes later, Municipal Judge Leland Lazarus, somewhat apologetically and on different grounds, issued the same order to his jury in the case against three defendants from the Condor. He directed a not guilty verdict for reasons entirely within context of the trial. "The defense," he said, "offered uncontradicted testimony that Miss Carol Doda's act did not violate community standards of decency."

After 90 minutes of deliberation, the Condor jury returned to the courtroom and asked for more instructions as to what the "moral standards of the community" are.

Obviously astonished, Judge Lazarus replied: "I'm sorry. I can't tell you what they are. But as far as the court is concerned, the prosecution has not proven in any way a violation of the standards.

"I have done a lot of soul-searching in this case and this is the first time in my five years on the bench that I have advised a jury to bring in an acquittal."

Foreman Nathan H. Davis then told the court the jury had already taken three ballots and was in disagreement.

"No matter how you do it," the judge replied, "whether reluctantly or not, you must bring in a verdict of not guilty."

45 minutes later, the jury filed into the courtroom and returned a verdict of acquittal for Carol Doda, Pete Mattioli, and Gino Del Prete.

Later the jury stated that at one time they were split five to seven. When they were polled for their verdict, four said they agreed to it "under protest."

Judges Direct Verdict

TOPLESS GALS FREED

San Francisco Examiner
MONARCH OF THE DAILIES
AMERICA FIRST
FINAL
SATURDAY, MAY 8, 1965

'Topless'--Back To The Old Grind

Topless Girls Freed-- Judges Direct Verdict

THE JUDGE ADVISED—AND 12 JURORS QUICKLY CONSENTED
Yvonne d'Angers (l.), Vori Barato, Marilyn Cutler and Kay Star

JUDGE LAZARUS
A directed verdict

JUDGE FRIEDMAN
A precedent

CAROL DODA
"Not guilty"

The Other Cases?

Negotiations On Seamen's War Bonus

s Girls Judges Verdict

North Beach Trials End

By JACK IVER

LESS PROMPT

The defendants and most of the audiences in both courtrooms reacted with jubilee—cheers, hugs, and back slaps. Within 45 minutes, show business at the Off Broadway returned to its particular brand of normality for the cocktail hour.

Pete Mattioli and Gino Del Prete returned to the Condor and quickly ordered a free round of drinks for all inside the club. Carol returned to her dressing room to get ready for the show that night, sans bra top. The North Beach topless scene resumed with gusto.

Charges were still pending against owners and performers of several clubs ....

District Attorney John Jay Ferdon said he would drop the remaining, pending prosecutions against the ten other club owners and a score of their female entertainers. He stated that in view of the decisions of the courts and expressed opinions of the juries, his office will move for dismissals. "This office finds these matters vulgar and distasteful. But we will be guided by what the courts have done," he said.

Police Chief Thomas J. Cahill stated, "We will continue to police the entire area, including all these North Beach premises. This is our duty. Company commanders and personnel will carry out their policing responsibilities. In addition, specialized units will continue the enforcement of law and general policing."

Most establishments resumed their bare-breasted entertainment after police officials made it abundantly clear that, in view of the verdicts, they had no intentions of conducting further raids at this time.

Said Inspector Thomas Fitzpatrick, director of intelligence and special services, when asked about future raids: "I wouldn't think it was expedient to do anything at this point. That is not a long-range promise, but no raids are planned for the immediate future."

The next day, Mayor John F. Shelley solemnly conceded that the courts have spoken loud and clear on the topless situation in North Beach. The Mayor, who once declared, "fun is part of our city's heritage," delivered his remarks with thoughtful resignation after learning that two Municipal Court judges had ordered juries to acquit the topless defendants and their employers. San Francisco Police Chief Tom Cahill declined to comment.

Despite Judge Friedman and Judge Lazarus's precedent-setting rulings, there were signs that the foes of bare-breasted performers were not ready to drop their banners.

Even as the jury was deliberating, an aide notified Voss Boreta, handsome proprietor of the Off Broadway, that the Alcoholic Beverage Control Department had filed charges against him and his brother, Chris, proprietor of The Cellar.

They had violated their liquor licenses, the ACBD declared, by acts contrary to public welfare and morals.

Raymond Stonehouse, ABCD area administrator, said his department objected particularly to topless employees co-mingling with patrons.

"That, by God, is persecution," snorted Melvin Belli when informed of the new charges. "Hallinan and I will move into court with so many writs it will look like snow falling over there."

The ABCD eventually dropped all topless related charges against the clubs.

16

Carol Quits!

"T OPLESS ACQUITTED!" screamed the front-page headlines of the Saturday, May 8, 1965 edition of *the San Francisco Chronicle.* "COURT FREES GIRLS" Inside it read, "TOPLESS – BACK TO THE OLD GRIND."

"TOPLESS GALS FREED!" read the banner above the masthead of the *San Francisco Examiner* that same day. "JUDGES DIRECT VERDICT."

Most people were stunned that the judges in each case had decided to direct their juries to return verdicts of exoneration. How it was that the jury was not able to decide the cases on their own was quite a mystery to some. But it was legal and it was done. Case closed.

Davey Rosenberg was right again. The trial verdicts produced madness on the North Beach topless scene as people were no longer uneasy to partake in all the fun goings on down there. If you got into one of the most popular clubs, it was after waiting in line, sometimes for more than an hour.

Playboy published an article in the April 1965 issue written by Herbert Gold, titled "The New Barbary Coast" and giving the nation a glimpse of what was happening in the Wild, Wild West club scene. Quoting Mr. Gold, "Conspicuously cantilevered Carol Doda, shown very much in the swim of things, is a pioneer held by West Coasters in equal esteem with

Pike, Fremont, the Forty-Niners, and Lily Langtry. Miss Doda (39-26-36) was the very first of the swim girls to don designer Rudi Gernreich's topless bathing suit. No dumb Dodo, Carol knew a good thing when she didn't see it. She has been a major attraction at the strip's Condor Club ever since. Her breast strokes have done more to popularize the latest swim suits than Eleanor Holm and Esther Williams combined."

Carol was asked in an interview if she worried about the silicone injections causing health problems. She responded by saying that she wasn't worried, that the tissue grows around it in a short period of time. She admitted that her breasts do feel different, however. Due to the added weight involved, she must wear a special heavy brassiere. She said that it was very uncomfortable to sleep on her stomach and on her side; she had to sleep on her back. She added that she works out with weights at the gym to build up her pectoral muscles to help support her breasts.

Herb Caen, in the *San Francisco Chronicle*, November 9, 1965, commented, "Internal Revenue is about to come face-to-face with a ticklish situation. On her next return, Carol Doda plans to deduct the cost of her silicone injections—$1,500—as a business expense. Or is it a capital gain?"

The Condor continued to book rock'n'roll shows such as Rik and the Ravens, featuring go-go girls such as Dori Lane and Pat Rose, but Carol remained the leading attraction. She was garnering national attention, especially after the trial verdicts, with several widespread publications comparing her to Jayne Mansfield and Mamie Van Doren.

Other things were evolving as well. Davey decided to begin the entertainment earlier in the evening, at 8:45 P.M. and feature 45-minute shows.

Meanwhile, some of North Beach's rowdiest crowd had been sent to San Quentin State Prison for such crimes as gambling or possession of a marijuana joint. After visiting one of his buddies in the prison, Davey thought it would be a grand idea to bring some lively entertainment to the prisoners. He booked "George and Teddy and the Condors featuring Carol Doda" to perform at the entertainment center of the prison. The group received an enthusiastic welcome, especially when Carol took the stage. The inmates stood, cheered, and whistled in full pandemonium. Fully clothed, she performed her song, dance, and comedy routine for the inmates, a night they certainly never forgot.

Pete and Gino were looking to hire a doorman/bouncer who could deal with some of the problems they were experiencing at the club. Lucky Lucchesi, the local, burly former Merchant Marine cook, was hired as bouncer at the Condor. He didn't get the job due to his good looks or his diplomatic handling of problems with clientele: he was hired because just seeing his gnarly face and looking into his glaring eyes would scare the hell out of most people. Standing an imposing six-feet-four-inches and weighing over 240 pounds, this nasty hulk of a man was one you would definitely want on your side. The scars and bulbous nose sprawled across the middle of his face would tell you that he was serious about his job and wasn't afraid of a knuckle sandwich.

Lucky bragged that he had been involved in over two hundred fights. When he escorted someone to the exit door, one usually heard loud screams, breaking glasses, splintering chairs, and toppling tables. Once out, the customer never tried to reenter. Lucky kept the order.

Lucky was sitting with Billy Breslin one day when he watched a couple of guys pick up a chair from the sidewalk café and walk down the street with it. Lucky and Billy jumped up in chase, but hadn't noticed the third man with them. He "copped a Sunday on" (punched) Lucky, and the next thing Lucky was aware of, he was lying in a bed at San Francisco General Hospital, proving that he was not invincible.

Lucky and Enrico eventually had a falling out. Enrico later confided that he didn't have any fights at his establishment after Lucky left.

Gino wanted to hire his friend, let's call him "Sam Pardini," as bartender at the Condor. Pete was against the idea, and since he was in charge of hiring and firing, he told Gino no, he didn't trust him.

"But he's my kid's godfather," Gino told Pete. "He really needs a job."

Pete relented and Pardini began bartending at the Condor.

One night, Pete saw a $40 tray of drinks go out and Sam only rang up $5. He watched more carefully and it happened again.

Pete confronted Gino. "Hey, Sam is stealing from us!" I saw him ring up $5 for a $40 tray of drinks."

"Oh, I forgot to tell you. I gave him the right to take ten bucks a day," Gino explained.

"Look, Gino," Pete began, his face reddening. "Number one, how do you know when he's got $10? And number two, who gave you the right to give him $5 of mine? He could have $100 and say he's only got $10. If you don't fire him, I will."

Sam was fired the next day.

One of the cops on the North Beach beat was Tommy Ryan, also known as "Tailspin Tommy," a name he earned during his high school football days as the kicker on the team.

One day as Pete was at the club setting up the bar, Tommy came running through the door shouting, "Come here, Pete, I want to show you something!" He ran out of the club and jogged across the street with Pete not far behind.

Officer Ryan ran into the Columbus Hotel, which was kitty-cornered from the Condor. Pete followed Tommy up the stairs. Tommy opened the door to a room and shoved Pete inside. A dead man was hanging from a rope. His face was blue, with saliva running from his mouth and snot dripping from his nose. He had a bowel movement lodged inside his pants and the room stank like shit.

Pete was speechless and frightened by the horrendous sight of the dangling man. As Pete stared in shock, Tommy laughed uncontrollably at his success in stunning his friend. Pete chased Tommy down the stairs and back to the club screaming obscenities at him the whole way.

Tony Cannistraci, the Condor's main bartender, asked if he could buy into the club. Tony didn't have any money to buy in, but Pete and Gino trusted him and knew he was honest. He looked after the business as if it was his own and they knew he would be a good partner.

They agreed to give Tony a ten percent interest in the club and he could pay them back with his ten percent of the proceeds. Tony took over many management responsibilities such as keeping the bar stocked, scheduling the cocktail waitresses, and making sure everything ran smoothly. He was handsome, dependable, well liked, and very cool. Giving Tony an interest in the club gave Pete some relief from the day-to-day operations. Tony became very important to their success.

It wasn't long before Carol had decided that to be a full-fledged star, she had to sing as well as dance during her act. Whether Carol could sing well or not really didn't matter, as no one ever paid entrance into the Condor to hear her sing. They paid to see her boobs and sexy body gyrate in moves they had never witnessed before. She did the Swim, the Twist, the Jerk, the Hully Gully—all the latest dances. And then there were her boobs. She was beautiful and erotic. The customers sat through her excruciatingly loud performances just to say they had seen Carol Doda. That's what they wanted to tell their friends when they got back to home. Watching her perform topless was the most important reason for them to be there. However, Carol wanted to learn to sing. She began taking singing lessons from Judy Davis, a dance and vocal coach, who had worked with the likes of Barbra Streisand, Vicki Carr, and the Kingston Trio. Carol began to improve her vocals and enhanced her dance routines.

Carol had a big, brash voice. Her voice was sometimes described as sounding like a cross between Ethel Merman and Marilyn Monroe, fluctuating between the two. She was not what you could call a natural born singer, but she worked very hard at improving her vocals by taking thousands of dollars' worth of singing lessons. She was determined to have respect as a singer as well as a dancer.

The one thing that no one disagreed with was that Carol's voice was loud. Extremely loud. In addition, Carol insisted on having the volume of the huge black speakers turned up high.

"Carol, for Christ's sake! Turn it down," Pete would yell over the pulsating music.

"I've got to hear myself," Carol would scream back.

Pete fought a constant battle with her over the sound volume. Sometimes patrons in the first few rows were seen covering their ears. Pete would tell Carol what the customers were doing, and she would just reply that the volume had to be loud so that she could hear herself. Case closed.

The volume controls were originally located next to the stage within easy reach of the performers. Carol could turn up the volume whenever she wanted by just walking over and adjusting the knobs. Time after time, she would turn the volume up and Pete would turn it back down. Finally, Pete got tired of fighting the volume battle with Carol and moved the speaker volume controls to the office in the basement of the building.

Carol would just go down when no one was around or send someone down to adjust the volume for her. So Pete came up with another plan.

Pete purchased several large black towels at a linen shop downtown. He removed the speaker covers and stuffed the towels, one by one, into the gigantic black speakers. "Aha. That should do the trick," he thought.

For two or three weeks, Carol complained that there was something wrong with the speakers. Her voice was sounding muffled to her, and she kept asking Pete to have the speakers fixed.

When Pete came to work the next day, he saw Carol standing on a chair pulling the black towels out of the speakers and throwing them on the floor. She was livid.

"What the fuck do you think you're doing?" demanded Carol. "You're ruining my career! I can't sing if I can't hear myself sing."

"We can hear you all the way up to Stockton Street!" Pete shouted. "It's so loud, we can't even hear the drink orders from the cocktail waitresses at the bar. You're driving people out of here. Doesn't it tell you something when you see people sticking their fingers in their ears and covering their ears with their hands?"

"Screw you!" she shrieked. "You let me run my show or I'm out of here."

The argument continued, punctuated by a few more swear words and screaming. But Carol pretty much won out on the volume arguments and the music reverted to being as loud as before.

On Tuesday, December 14, 1965, Carol gyrated through what she said was her final performance at the Condor.

"There must be more to life than this," she was quoted as saying, "and I hope to find out."

After the show, the Queen of Topless emptied the dressing of her belongings, packed them into a suitcase, and marched out of the club.

"I quit!" she yelled to Pete, who was sitting at the bar.

Carol was hired to perform in several clubs located in Las Vegas and Hollywood, but didn't draw much of a crowd outside her hometown. The glittering entertainment productions in Vegas had already gone "topless" and the quality of talent in Los Angeles was deep and wide-ranging.

The audiences dismissed Carol's appearances as just another bare-breasted boobie show.

The "Direct from San Francisco" headline didn't work in Las Vegas in the same way as "Direct from Las Vegas" worked in San Francisco.

Meanwhile, Davey Rosenberg quickly hired a fresh new topless dancer, twenty-one-year-old Margo Sweet, to strut her stuff at the Condor. He promoted her appearance as "Direct from Las Vegas." Davey publicized her arrival by placing a topless photo of her in the display case outside of the club. The State Alcohol and Beverage Control Department threatened to suspend their liquor license unless they removed the bare-chested photos. The Off Broadway was also cited for topless photo advertising outside the club. Both clubs quickly covered the bare boobs with bikini tops.

Scrambling to attract customers after Carol left, Davey came up with another gimmick to draw the crowd into the Condor. He ordered several New York–made foundation corsets for the cocktail waitresses to wear. One was red, white, and blue with stars around the waist and red stripes running from the waist to the crotch. Another had two huge eyes painted on the backside bottom and another was white with a huge black zipper running from the waist to the crotch. They were bottom-only creations and worn over black leotards.

Davey had found them on sale at Gray Reid's in Reno and thought they would be a hit at the club.

"Send me all you got," Davey told them. The cost was $56, cheap for all the publicity they received, photos and stories published in the *Examiner* and other publications.

The Daughters of the American Revolution protested the new outfits, calling them unpatriotic and risqué. The girls thought they were a novelty and fun to wear. "What is the DAR, anyway?" was the question they floated around the club.

Davey hired The Checkmates, who were regular performers at Harvey's Casino in Reno and Caesar's Palace Casino in Las Vegas. The Checkmates were a mixed-race group of very seasoned entertainers and were wildly popular on the West Coast. Singing songs from the Top 40 charts such songs as "Louie Louie," "Baby, I Need Your Lovin'," and "You've Lost That Lovin' Feelin'," they filled the Condor to capacity at each performance.

Yvonne D'Angers being chained to the Golden Gate Bridge by Davey Rosenberg to avoid deportation.

On New Year's Eve, 1965, Pete decided to forgo a cover charge at the door of the Condor and institute a two-drink minimum. They had a twenty-minute show with a ten-minute break to clear the room and fill the seats again. This policy was unheard of on the street, and set a new precedent.

Voss Boreta, owner of the Off Broadway, was furious, not only that the Condor did not charge a cover at the door, but also that they could institute a new show every 30 minutes. Within a few weeks, every topless club changed over to the new format of 20-minute shows and a two-drink minimum. Many club owners simply copied what the Condor owners did as Pete, Gino, and Davey were considered the pacesetters on the street.

Pete was unaware that Davey was also working as a promoter for the Off Broadway, but soon found out after Yvonne D'Angers, star attraction at that venue, received a deportation notice from the U.S. Department of Immigration. She had caught the attention of the authorities due to her obscenity trial. Davey came up with the crazy idea of chaining her to the Golden Gate Bridge to avoid deportation. The press turned out in droves for the bizarre spectacle, and the Off Broadway club was filled to capacity each night. Deportation efforts never succeeded, but the Golden Gate escapades paid off and resulted in several movie contracts for Miss D'Angers.

In January 1966, the Condor introduced a novel new act on the stage at the improbable hour of noon. Linda Lee Scott descended on the piano wearing a skimpy topless tiger outfit, her face painted like a cat. Suddenly dancer Alberto Marco, also in tiger motif, wearing a flapping sleeveless vest and slit leather trousers, jumps catlike onto the piano from the hole in the ceiling. Bare-breasted female meets bare-chested man. It was inevitable. They danced around each other for a few minutes and then up, up, they went disappearing back into the ceiling.

Standing by for the act was the Condor attorney, Harry Wainwright, who stated, "The issue is not whether it offends someone, but rather whether the production is legally obscene. It's considered artistic expression," he continued, "and as such, is protected under the Constitution as freedom of expression."

The act was scheduled for the evening performance and was a huge hit. It brought additional great publicity and more long lines around the block for the Condor. Davey Rosenberg had done it again.

Some of the longstanding North Beach venues began to complain that the topless clubs were stealing business that should be theirs. Enrico Banducci, owner of the hungry i, and Bee Goman, owner of Goman's Gay 90's, complained that they were losing customers to the strip- and topless clubs. A meeting was held at the Off Broadway, owned by Chris and Voss Boreta, in which they called in their attorney, Harry Wainwright.

"People have gotten tired of the old routines that Bee Goman has been putting on for decades. It's time she retired," Chris said. Pete and Gino agreed.

Everything was changing on the street, and some of the old timers were being left out of the action.

Pete heard that Dick Boyd wanted to sell his half interest in Pierre's nightclub just up the street from the Condor. Looking to expand his interests in the North Beach entertainment district, Pete bought it and became a partner with Maurice Bessiere in Pierre's.

Lesbian Tommy Vasu, known on the street as "Tommy the Dyke," came into Pierre's often to play liar's dice. Walter Keane loved playing liar's dice, and often challenged Tommy to a match. Wearing a double-breasted suit topped by a fedora, she was usually accompanied by her beautiful blonde girlfriend. Tommy owned the parking concession between New Joe's and Enrico's, a very lucrative business. She also owned Tommy's Joint at 529 Broadway and 12 Adler, a famous lesbian hangout. Tommy was well liked around the neighborhood and was considered just another figure of the diverse North Beach crowd.

Tommy's girlfriend got hooked on heroin and Tommy did all she could to keep her supplied. She started dealing, and the homophobic SFPD was more than happy to arrest her. The evidence was flimsy, but Tommy didn't wait for a trial. She made bail and became a fugitive. After eventually turning herself in, she was sentenced to five years prison time at the California Correctional Institution in Tehachapi.

❖ ❖ ❖

Carol returned from Las Vegas, moseying back into the Condor wearing golden Capri pants and a straining blouse. She sat down at a cocktail table, brooding.

"Like in Vegas, who needs it," Carol mused. "They've got bosoms on top of bosoms."

The Silver Slipper, a famous striptease venue, had hired her, but she quickly learned that there were hundreds of beautiful women working the strip. She was competing with experienced strip artists with elaborate costumes.

"There they were stripping," Miss Doda recalled, "and I came on already stripped."

She resisted the blandishments of the management to become a stripper and looked, instead, for other opportunities. Soon she was back at the Condor asking for her job back.

Pete rehired her and she returned to the piano on February 3, 1966. The reaction from topless enthusiasts was tremendous. In addition to Carol returning, the topless male-and-female act continued to perform. The club was packed to the rafters nightly once again.

Competition had increased in the neighborhood, though, as Pete had hired a young stripper named Sandy Simmons to perform at his new club, Pierre's. In her act, she attached tassels to her nipples and was able to twirl them in opposite directions.

It was debated as to whether Carol's silicone breasts could strike twice. She knew she needed to up her act, and signed up for more vocal lessons. In the meantime, she opted for more silicone injections, and her breast size increased to 44 inches.

Davey Rosenberg resumed his role as top promoter of all things Carol Doda and booked her for an appearance at University of California's Sproul Plaza promoting a charity event titled the "Ugly Man Contest." The report in the March 3, 1966, *San Francisco Chronicle* described the event this way:

> The collective minds of UC students were completely diverted from issues such as the Vietnam War, civil rights, and free speech by the 44-inch bust of Miss Doda. The usual political action on the plaza was completely forgotten. Around 6,000 google-eyed students cheered "hurrahs" as the silicone-reinforced topless

star wiggled on the balcony to the tune of "Gypsy Tale." A fire and brimstone message being delivered at the nearby Bancroft Gate by Evangelist Hubert Lindsey was completely drowned out.

Lindsey, robbed of his usual noontime audience, turned his eyes away from the gyrating dancer with a bitter comment. "It's Satanic; it's against scripture," he said.

Three lonely Nazis parading at the gate were also eclipsed by the Doda exhibition and marched away in a kind of superman huff.

Miss Doda wore white stretch pants, a white "Batman" T-shirt, and high-heeled white boots for her rock'n'roll invasion of the Berkeley campus.

Ostensibly, she appeared there as a candidate for the Ugly Man crown, a freshman class fundraising contest to support Cal Camp for the underprivileged children.

Thousands of students wrestling with algebraic equations, translations of Greek couplets, and life swarmed around her on the Sproul Hall steps. They hung from balconies, crowded onto rooftops, sprouted from the trees.

The Cal Band was on hand, too, braced to pipe the topless wonder into action.

As it turned out, however, there was not enough room on the steps for Miss Doda to fully exercise her talents. That's when she retreated to the second floor balcony where she performed alone—a tiny figure prancing before thousands of upraised eyes.

It was clear that she was the favorite but would indeed make a funny looking "Ugly Man." She didn't win the contest.

A generously endowed actress and stripper, Tura Satana, was another Condor dancer at the time. William Gilkerson interviewed her in the *Datebook*, a *San Francisco Chronicle* publication, on Sunday, March 27, 1966:

> Webster's Unabridged Dictionary defines a tassel as "a pendant ornament, ending in a tuft of loose threads of cords, attached to the corners of cushions, curtains, and the like."

This is a good description of the tassels worn by Tura, the Topless Tassel Twirler, currently twirling at the Condor. Tura's tassels are tufted, they are indeed ornamental, and, being attached directly to her person, they are the like.

"I put them on with spirit gum," she explained as she sat in a dark corner of the Condor. "It's the same stuff they use to fasten wigs and toupees. Once one came off and flew into a lady's drink."

Tura (who is billed in full as Tura Satana) is Japanese, is well mannered, has black tresses, a soft voice, and fulsome twirling equipment. Her between-shows costume was a dark wraparound dress that parted slightly at the bosom when she leaned forward.

"My act is never offensive to anybody," she said, leaning forward, "because I just kid around. It's not really sexy at all. Just watch. I'm going on now."

Watching Tura in action, one learns that there is more to tassel twirling than meets the eye. Not only can the tassels be twirled clockwise, in unison, but in the merest instant the action can be reversed and a counter-clockwise motion established. They can also be set going in opposite directions, and, as a kind of finale, one can be stopped dead, while the other continues to spin.

During much of her twirling, Tura leans casually against the piano, chatting at random with the drummer or individuals in the audience. She also plays a passable Bossa Nova on the cymbals with her tassels (while someone in the band does bird calls), and it should probably be pointed out in passing that these tassels glow in the dark.

After her act, she suggested the chat be continued in the dressing room. "It's less distracting there," she said. "Fewer people."

And sure enough, there were just two other people there— Carol Doda in only a G-string, and Paula, the Topless Tigress, in the same.

Tura brushed her hair as she continued: "I was born in Japan, came to this country when I was five, and started stripping when I was fourteen."

Where did she learn to twirl tassels?

"I taught myself, but a number of women who have seen my act have asked me to teach them. Once I asked one why she wanted to learn. 'For parties,' she told me. Another time a guy wanted me to teach him. 'Where are you going to put them?' I asked him. Incidentally, I hope you're not offended by any of this. I always seem to talk more freely in the dressing room."

"This is our social outlet room," put in Carol Doda. "We think everybody should have a social outlet room. We say anything up here. Wanna hear some of the things we say?" she challenged.

How about teaching Carol to twirl tassels?

"Not me," said Carol. "Mine don't even move anymore."

"A lot of people ask me if twirling won't cause sag," continued Tura, "but it's really the best way to prevent it. It's very good exercise. More women should do it."

"I never exercised mine," said Carol, applying lipstick, "I just kept on getting shots."

"Look, said Tura, slipping off her robe. "The action all comes from the pectoral muscles, like this." She demonstrated.

"If I did that," observed Carol, "It would be positively grotesque."

"This dressing room," said Tura, pressing ahead, is like a Fellini film. Don't you think? Fellini's one of my favorite directors. I'd like to play in one of his movies."

Films that Tura has in fact played in include *Irma la Douce* and *Our Man Flint*. Another, entitled *Faster Pussycat, Kill! Kill!* featured Tura in a starring role.

"I've also done a lot of TV work. I really prefer movies and TV to twirling or exotic dancing." This led into a discussion of definitions.

"Technically," she pointed out, "an exotic dancer is an Oriental dancing girl who doesn't strip. But, of course, she's nearly nude to begin with. Your strippers start out dressed to the teeth and do away with it all gradually. Go-go dancers wear a bikini or some kind of creeping skirt and do the Jerk, Swim, Watusi, or any of the others like that. A tassel twirler, of course, just twirls her tassels."

For relaxation, Tura works out at aikido and writes love poetry. "I also read a lot. I like Plato, Dante, and Boswell. But in reading Boswell, I get the impression that he was very confused. Then sometimes I just like to go sit in a corner by myself. Away from people. And then, too, I watch a lot of TV. Nobody watches more TV than I do.

"Oh yes," said Carol, "me. I even watch test patterns."

And what did Tura ever do about that guy who wanted to learn twirling . . . did she teach him?

"No. I could have, though. But I couldn't have taught him to twirl as well as I do. Let's face it, I have more leverage."

Even though the well-dressed nighttime crowds continued to frequent the North Beach entertainment district, there were more and more complaints about the increase in crime.

While employed as a bouncer at the Condor, tough guy Joe Purple was "worked over" by five thugs from the Peninsula and ended up at St. Francis Memorial Hospital. A hearing was held with the Board of Supervisors, including Peter Tamaras, chairman, George Moscone, John Ertola, Joseph Casey, and Roger Boas. Appearing at the hearing were Capt. Charles Barca of Central District, Deputy Chief Al Arnaud, and Police Commissioner William P. Clecak. The police officers told the supervisors that crime was indeed up in the area, with arrests up 90% and major crimes up 25%.

It was agreed that more officers were needed in North Beach, but the police reminded them that if they place more officers in the area, they might not be able to respond to a major emergency or fire in another area. A formal report of fire hazards and traffic flows was requested, but nothing was done at the time.

Anthony "Coke" Infante, former owner of the Condor, was still floating around North Beach, cruising the scene in his white Jaguar. One night while he was in the Condor and just feeling mean, he decided to rouse up Hommy Stewart, a midget who made his living as maître d' and house photographer at some of the clubs. Standing less than four feet tall, Hommy was a likable guy, but Coke decided to have some fun and rough him up a bit. Coke threw some judo chops at Hommy, kicked him in the stomach, picked him up, and threw him to the floor. Hommy ended up in the hospital and threatened to sue Coke for $40,000. After a complete check-up at the hospital, Hommy was released with no injuries. His threatened lawsuit never materialized.

D avey Rosenberg decided that it was time for Carol to take her awesome 44-inch bust and groovy dance moves to New York City. Carol relished the mission to show those poor struggling topless girls in the Big Apple what it's all about.

The topless craze had already been introduced by the bare-bosomed waitresses at the Crystal Room on 54th Street and the Village West in Greenwich Village. Mayor John V. Lindsay was not as enthusiastic about the West Coast art form and ordered a change in cabaret regulations, banishing all topless costumes for waitresses. He gave the venues 24 hours to comply.

Two topless waitresses, Ruby Diamond and Mary Rooney, had already been arrested for indecent exposure but were released into the custody of their attorneys. They were scheduled for a hearing on December 7, 1966, which was expected to ultimately result in Manhattan's first topless trial.

Carol learned that the New York girls were wearing pasties, a shocking compromise.

"Pasties!" she declared. "You can't call that topless!"

Carol wanted to attend the topless trials, as an "observer," or as a witness if she might be called to testify.

"I mean," explained Miss Doda, "I've had experience. I was arrested once."

Pete, Carol, and Davey Rosenberg flew to New York and were met with lavish enthusiasm. They met up with celebrities at Jilly's, Frank Sinatra's hangout, and dined at the 21 Club. Carol met several star personalities including Joe Namath, quarterback for the New York Jets.

They visited a couple of "topless" clubs, but Carol never actually performed in New York. The trip ended up being just a big publicity stunt cooked up by Davey Rosenberg. They all concluded that New York

Doting Daddy Pete.

entertainment scene was a hard nut to crack, so they returned to San Francisco without any increase in Carol's profile.

Back in San Francisco, Davey continued booking Carol at events around the Bay Area and was determined to portray her as a good citizen who just happened to be a topless dancer. He wanted her to be accepted within the community. She appeared as Queen of the Grand Prix in Cotati, where some of the nation's top drivers competed for National Championship Sports Car racing points.

She dished out mounds of mashed potatoes and juicy hunks of meat on board the *USS Enterprise* while the world's largest aircraft carrier was docked at the San Francisco Naval Shipyard. The chow-line waitress received no complaints about the meal—it could have been mush or hash and the sailors could not have cared less.

"Any breast of chicken?" asked one sailor.

"Very funny," said Miss Doda.

Afterward, Carol captained a softball team put together of other topless wonders from the Condor, who challenged the Big E's Nuclear Power team at Funston Playground, dramatizing support for Armed Forces relief funds.

Davey placed a coupon in the *Chronicle* asking for readers to state their support for Carol Doda to visit the boys in Vietnam. He asked readers to mail the coupon back to him at the Condor. A total of 12 coupons were returned.

And once again, *Playboy* featured the Condor and the hottest star in North Beach, Carol Doda, this time in the September, 1966 issue in an article on the Topless Revolution (Yvonne d'Angers was seen as well).

For any number of good reasons, Pete decided to isolate his family from the crazy life of North Beach and move out of the City. He had a five-year-old daughter, Amy, and had adopted his wife's teenage son from her previous marriage, Chris. He began commuting to the City after purchasing a home in Millbrae. Later he bought a six-bedroom home on two acres in Novato. He bought a pony named King for Amy and a drum set for Chris. But his marriage was falling apart due to the long hours working at the Condor and the party life that was prevalent. Pete would arrive home sometimes after four or five a.m. to an angry wife who, quite reasonably, felt neglected. They argued about the care and discipline of the children. Life on Broadway was wild and uncontrolled, with heavy drinking involved in daily activities. He and Arlene fought often and hard through alcohol-fueled arguments. They divorced in 1967.

Arlene was originally awarded custody of both children, but Pete wasn't happy with that arrangement. He asked his sister and brother-in-law, Elaine and Harold Loosigian, if they would be willing to have Amy live with them and their two children in Fresno. Pete's mother, Elena, also lived there. He wanted Amy to have a more secure family life, which he wasn't able to provide at the time. Pete asked for another hearing and requested custody of his daughter. Arlene relinquished full custody to Pete, and Amy was welcomed into his sister's home. He made a point of driving to Fresno every two weeks to visit her. At the age of sixteen, Amy moved to Santa Rosa to be with her dad and me.

Since things were running quite smoothly at the Condor, Pete decided to join some of his North Beach friends who were planning a trip to Europe. Art Benjamin, Maurice Bessiere, Voss Boreta, and Joe Engarcia invited Pete to travel with them to England and France. Throngs of family and friends gathered on the tarmac at the San Francisco International Airport to see the group off on their journey.

Upon arrival at London's Heathrow Airport, customs officials cast their suspicious eyes upon the club operators and pulled them aside. Immigration officers confiscated their passports and put them in a holding room for questioning. They seemed to think that the topless club owners were planning to open topless venues in their fair city.

After two-and-a-half hours of relentless interrogation from the officials, the group was able to convince the authorities that they were just tourists. The officials returned their passports and told them to have a lovely time visiting London.

That night they called a taxi to explore the City's nightlife. They asked the driver if he could suggest a nightclub where they could find some fun. He took them to a gentlemen's club where most of the entertainment was, ahem, nude!

While in Monaco, the San Francisco trekkers were exploring the waterfront when they came upon a gorgeous new yacht and saw that it was named *Westlake*. It was owned by Henry Doelger, a San Francisco developer known for creating large housing tracts featuring small, low-cost, box-like homes in San Francisco's Sunset District, Westlake District, and Daly City. He was one of the richest people in the Bay Area.

Doelger spotted the group, recognized them, and invited them onboard. As they were enjoying a cocktail and getting a tour of the impressive new yacht, they noticed a good-looking couple standing on the dock admiring the boat. It turned out to be Elizabeth Taylor and Richard Burton. They were impressed by what they saw, and requested to come aboard. Doelger graciously accommodated them, showing them around and introducing them to the boys from San Francisco.

That night they had some fun at a couple of houses of prostitution. It was easy to find exciting adult entertainment in Monaco. And topless clubs were everywhere!

17

Carol Doda's Nightclub

I t was June of 1968. Since Gino wasn't active in the management of
the Condor, he was itching to open another club. Over drinks with
Voss Boreta, they saw an opportunity to convince Carol that she was
not receiving her share of the proceeds from her work at the Condor.
They persuaded her to leave the Condor and partner with them to
open a club they would name after her, Carol Doda's. They told her
she would receive a percentage of the profits and would draw all the
action from the Condor. She agreed, packed up her act once again, and
walked down the street to 430 Broadway to the club that quickly bore
her name.

"You're invited to the kickiest scene ever," read the widely distributed
telegram. "Carol Doda does her thing at her own club. Live and on film,
she sings, dances, and emotes."

Robert Taylor, columnist for the *San Francisco Chronicle*, wrote:

> In her new show at 430 Broadway, she tries a number of clever
> disguises to fool us. The most ambitious is a judge's black gown
> and a tall white wig.
>
> But you can tell its Carol, as no other judge would walk into
> court in a topless robe.

She sings, and "emotes" ever so slightly in some filmed sequences, which make up about half of the show, but Carol the singer and Carol the actress are never as successful as Carol the body.

In a red satin bikini bottom and some sort of supporting top contraption, she sings, "I Left My Heart in San Francisco," while two boys in striped pants and satin shirts do some silly dances.

While she changes into a sequin dress to sing "The Story of Love," the boys dance to "Love for Sale."

Then the fellows jump into powder-blue plastic overalls and Miss Doda puts on a ragged skirt and a pair of sleeves for the country number, "A Real Live Boy."

Later, there is "Mame" in a topless gold lamé dress (will we have a topless "Mama" after the all-Negro cast?) and a topless "I Ain't Down Yet," from *The Unsinkable Molly Brown.*

Miss Doda's basically weak voice is heavily amplified, but she does seem to hit all the right notes.

More in attempted in the filmed sequences than is accomplished, but at least it shows some evidence of ingenuity in a nightclub routine.

The movie screen, about midway back on the small stage, is split like vertical venetian blinds, so Miss Doda and her two friends can leap from the film onto the stage and back again in a Keystone Kops chase.

Another sequence has topless Carol dancing on stage while a filmed close-up of topless Carol dancing spreads her figure across the screen.

Not until Cinerama goes topless will there be a bigger show in town.

Many people assumed that Carol actually owned part of the club that bore her name. But she didn't. Not on paper, anyway.

"They said they would give me a percentage, but they never did," she said in a later interview.

Carol was never paid very much for her performances either, as her partners got first count of the cash, and there wasn't much left for her.

When she questioned them about it, they retorted about how much her shows cost to produce and promote.

Even though her name was known throughout the entertainment world, it was connected to the Condor so strongly that she found that her name, Carol Doda, standing alone, wasn't enough to be successful.

July 7, 1972 – *San Francisco Examiner*

> State Alcoholic Beverage Control officials today gave the true owners of the Carol Doda nightclub at 430 Broadway in San Francisco 30 days to identify themselves or probably lose their liquor license.
>
> Yenrak, Inc. holds the license now, the ABC said. But the action is to determine whether Gino Del Prete and Josephine Belasco are the actual owners or part owners.
>
> The Alcoholic Beverage Control act prohibits ownership of a liquor establishment by "silent partners."

Carol Doda's, the club, eventually went broke and closed. The identity of the license holder was not made public.

Carol recalled in an April 28, 1986, *People Magazine* interview about her namesake club:

> The place was always packed, and I got a chance to do really interesting shows, like coming on in a Carmen Miranda outfit singing "The Girl from Ipanema" and then taking my top off.
>
> I never spoke a word in my act, until one night I looked out into the audience and saw a man who looked bored. Bored! That's when I opened my mouth and said, "What's the matter with you? You studying to be a monk or something?" After that, I started doing my one-liners. I don't think I've lasted this long just because I was up there taking my top off. I hope it's because people liked my sense of humor, too. I liked stripping, but I always liked to make them laugh first, and then take off my clothes.
>
> I've met some strange ones over the years. Like the blind couple from New York that came in to see the show. They said they were sight-seeing—that was the word they used—and that I was one of the focal points of their trip. After the show, the

woman asks, "Do you think my husband could have a feel of your breasts?" I mean, what do you say when a blind man asks to feel your breasts? I told them sorry, but it's against the law, which it was. I really think they were blind, though, and not just pretending so he could cop a feel.

Carol starred in a new production titled *Guru You*, a spoof on the sex films of the day. The show was a combination of both cinematic and the in-the-flesh talents of Miss Doda, using "push through the screen" techniques. The costuming ranged from gangsterish white striped suits to bell-bottoms, with some breakaway outfits that revealed much of her famous breasts.

Undeterred and determined to expand her resume and acting career, Carol made several other attempts, dabbling in a live stage performance and movies.

Carol Doda's much anticipated acting debut occurred when she appeared as Sadie Thompson in the drenchy old melodrama *Rain* at the Encore Theater. The play closed after four weeks and opinion was unanimous: the Queen of Topless had laid an egg. Audiences agreed that she was no actress and had no hidden talents on stage. They established that she was a sweet-looking thing, but her tarty role actually suited her personality.

A sadder but wiser lady, Carol resumed her acting classes at the American Conservatory Theater. The Condor offered her $500 per week to return to her piano, but she was not ready to return. She wanted to be a movie star.

She flew to Hollywood and accepted a bit part in a movie with Victor Mature and the Monkees titled *Head*. Her name in the flick: Sally Silicone. It flopped.

Back in San Francisco, producer Phil Oesterman cast Carol in a new production written by Gus Weill called *Geese*, which opened at the Encore Theater. Marking her second stab at legitimate theater, she consented to act the role of a lesbian.

"*Geese* is a step forward for me." Carol explained. "I chose *Geese* because it's a beautiful play, and it has something to say for today about love."

What made her role even more interesting is that she acted as the more mannish of the two lesbians. She played the aggressor in a nude love scene, which brought to play its erotic climax. Carol answered the question as to why she was cast as the butch member of the duo.

"Because," answered Carol, "I can't see myself in the other role of a girl who's been reared in the sheltered environment of a Southern plantation. While I don't know an awful lot about lesbians, I can understand the butch girl. She's been knocked around by life. And so have I."

"I'm fed up with topless," said Carol. "I was overworked and underpaid."

"This show will be funny and exciting and, best of all, it'll be a musical," Carol continued. "I'd like people to come with open minds and lots of love."

Geese actually evolved into two plays, the first starring Carol Doda as a bull dyke and the second about two gay men trying to figure a way to come out in front of one set of parents. It was called *Parents and Children*, and starred Charles Pierce, a well-known female impersonator. *Geese* was a calamity of nudity and hilariousness, but carried a message of love, acceptance, and understanding. It lasted about four months, but when it closed, Carol was out of work again.

Meanwhile, everything was still rockin' at the Condor. Topless entertainment was making wads of money for everyone on the street. Pete spent $25,000 to add another entrance to the Condor from Columbus Avenue, increasing exposure of the club to the street.

Professional golfer Ray Floyd was a regular at the Condor. Pete and Ray became friends, and Pete followed him on the golfing circuit, often playing golf with him. Everyone was amazed at Ray's skills at putting the ball exactly where he wanted it. One day, Ray bragged that he could hit the ball and it would go straight up into the air and come straight down to precisely where he hit it. Pete and the guys called on him to prove it, which he did. Ray could tell you how to make a ball curve to the left or right, travel up or down during flight, and so many other tricks.

On the other hand, Pete was a terrible golfer, having a handicap in the 30s. But he enjoyed the game, camaraderie, and friendships he established on the golf course.

Pete, Gino, and many of the other North Beach rounders took numerous trips to Las Vegas and Reno, where they were treated like celebrities by the management and pit bosses of the casinos. They gambled extravagantly, won some, and lost a lot.

Pete met Bill Harrah and the top management of Harrah's clubs, and became good friends with Holmes Hendricksen, manager of Harrah's. Pete was invited to participate in the yearly Harrah's celebrity golf tournaments, playing golf with Fred MacMurray, Joe DiMaggio, and many other celebrities. Bill Harrah would send his private jet to pick up the North Beach bunch at Butler Aviation at SFO. Upon arrival, they would be driven to the clubs in Rolls Royces with license plates HARRAH1, HARRAH2, etc. Of course, they paid for all this pampering by regularly dropping ten or twenty thousand dollars at the blackjack, craps, and poker tables. Pete's entire trip was "prepaid" by his gambling account, and he received VIP treatment throughout his stay. He was seated in the front row at all the shows, enjoyed complimentary dining and, of course, girls, girls, girls!

18

Girls, Girls, Girls

On September 3, 1969, Carol Doda removed her bikini bottom and danced completely nude at the Condor. Other dancers at the Condor and other clubs followed suit, much to the chagrin of the community and law enforcement.

"Hey, Pete," yelled one of the bottomless dancers from the upstairs dressing room. "Can you come up and help me out? I need a favor."

Pete scaled the stairs and entered the dressing room.

"Can you shave my pussy hairs into a heart?" she asked.

"Huh?" Pete stammered.

"Yeah, I want it shaped like a heart," she explained.

"Sure, let me try," Pete said. He pulled two chairs together and told her to stand on top of the chairs. She had some shaving cream and razor in hand, so he carefully began shaping her soft dark brown muff into a heart. Attentively, she watched in the mirror as he worked. "What do you think?" Pete inquired when he was done.

"I'd say it looks damned good!" she exclaimed. "Very pretty!"

Upon learning of the new pubic design, the other bottomless dancers debuted artistic designs of all kinds. There were diamond shapes, flower shapes, and complete shaves. The ladies attached flesh-colored tape that made them look similar to a mannequin and, therefore, more acceptable to the audience.

❖ ❖ ❖

Often the 2 a.m. closing time mandated by the Alcoholic Beverage Control Department was just the beginning of the party for many club owners. The beautiful showgirls from Bimbo's 360 Club on Columbus Avenue and the Moulin Rouge were regulars at these after-hours parties, as they had to stay sober for their performances but were ready for a few cocktails after their shift. They were ready to revel after work and the Condor was the hottest after-hours club—with a downstairs sex-pit office. Drinks were free flowing, and some indulged in a marijuana "stick" or two.

There was one San Francisco policeman, Officer McHenry, who agreed to lock the partygoers inside the club at 2 a.m. and unlock the door at the end of his night shift. The officer hung a huge padlock on the outside door, indicating that the club had closed up for the night. If any other police officers happened by and shined their flashlight on the door, they would assume that the club was unoccupied and locked up. When Officer McHenry got off work, he would return to the club, unlock the door, and give the lock to Pete or Gino. He never took a nickel or a drink for this service. He just liked to hang out at the club.

Most musicians at the Condor took their instruments home with them after their performances. But after Sam the Man and the Flintstones performed, Sam would leave his complete musical setup on stage. One night, Sean Connery and Buddy Greco were there at closing time and stuck around for after-hours fun. Some of the cocktail waitresses stayed as well. Sean grabbed the saxophone and made miserable attempts to play it. Gino blasted away on the trumpet, while Buddy, an accomplished jazz pianist and singer, played the famous piano in an impromptu jam session. It lasted until daylight. Pete, the consummate businessman and not a wannabe musician, sat at the office desk that night, counting the night's cash receipts.

❖ ❖ ❖

Davey backstage with topless and bottomless dancers.

The basement of the building housing the Condor was turned into an office when the major remodel had been done on the club in 1961. Besides service as an office, it was used as the audition room for dancers applying to work there. It was the perfect place for a private party.

As you descended the very steep staircase and turned left you entered a sizeable room. Directly on your left was a large desk. Underneath the stairs Pete had installed a safe behind a false wall covered in cork, a trendy wall covering at the time. The sound system with a reel-to-reel tape deck was installed inside the wall and used for auditions and private parties. The office speakers were mounted on the wall above the sound system at the back of the room.

Behind the desk was a door, which led to a bathroom complete with a shower big enough for two, and a six-person sauna room. To the right of the bathroom door there was a large dark brown leather couch, which sat along the brick wall. The rest of the room consisted of huge pillows, which filled the carpeted floor. There was another large safe placed at the other side of the room. A false ceiling was constructed to give the office a more intimate appearance. The downstairs office would comfortably accommodate about fifteen people. Interviews would go something like this:

"Hey, Pete! Got a job interview!" shouts Gino from the top of the stairwell leading down to the Condor basement office.

"Send her down," Pete responds.

"Go on down. He'll take care of you," Gino instructs the fashionably dressed, longhaired brunette.

Pete gathers up the cash from the top of his desk, stuffs it into a bank bag, and slides it into the desk drawer. He can hear someone's heels clomping as they make the sharp descent into the basement office.

The lovely face of an innocent looking young woman peeks from around the corner.

"Hi," she whispers.

"Come on in," Pete summons. "What's your name?"

"Susie," she murmurs.

"So you want a job?" Pete asks.

"Yeah, I mean, yes, I'm a dancer."

"OK, can I see your ID?" Pete responds.

She digs into her purse for her identification, coming up with a California driver's license, and hands it to Pete. It looks to Pete like the birth date had been altered to indicate she was 21 years old. He doesn't care, though, because according to the law, all he had to do was ask for an ID stating that she was 21. That was old enough to work in an establishment that sold alcohol.

"Alright, this will work," Pete determines. He reaches for the sound system controls, which were inside a cabinet under the stairs, and turns some music on.

"So, take off your clothes and let's see what you can do," Pete instructs.

"Huh?" she responds.

"Remove your clothes and dance a little for me," Pete repeats.

"Oh, yes, OK," Susie replies haltingly.

While she wriggles out of her clothes, Pete sits back in his chair and enjoys the view. This was certainly one of the best perks of his job.

"Panties, too?" she asks.

"Yup, panties too. You can keep your high heels on," Pete directs.

"Oh, thanks," Susie ekes out, with a shy smile.

Susie applies her most seductive face and begins to move. It is apparent that she was a good dancer, but this was quite unlike any job interview she has participated in. Susie does her best to perform in the small space allotted her for the interview, twisting, waterless swimming, and spinning. She dances to a few songs until Pete finally says, "OK, that's good. We'll give you a chance."

Thrilled and relieved, Susie nearly collapses on Pete's desk. He takes her arm and steadies her as she whispers a thank you.

"Have a seat," Pete offers, gesturing towards the couch. "You can put your clothes back on now."

"Thank you, Mr. Mattioli," she responds, as she gathers her belongings and takes a seat on the couch.

"So, you're from Modesto?" Pete tries to ease into conversation.

"Yes, have you ever been there?" she responds.

"I've driven through Modesto many times to visit my daughter in Fresno. She lives with my sister and mother," Pete answers, taking a seat beside her on the couch.

Dressed and feeling more comfortable now, Susie sits back and relaxes a bit. Pete offers her a drink from his private bar.

"I'd like a Manhattan," she states.

"Hey, I like Manhattans too," Pete replies as he mixes up the drinks.

Pete explains the "house rules" to Susie as she listens intently and sips her drink.

1. You must be on time for all performances.
2. You must be totally sober to perform.
3. Topless and bottomless dancing are restricted to the stage.
4. No touching the clientele at any time, going to or coming from the stage.

Susie agrees to all the rules, and asks if there was any rule against dating the boss.

"Nope, no rules like that," Pete clarifies.

"That's just fine with me," Susie says as she locks eyes with Pete.

Soon Susie's clothes are off again and on the floor. The job interview was complete.

❖　❖　❖

S ometimes the job interviews, if one could call them interviews, oc-curred at the Greyhound Bus Station down on 5th and Market Street. Young girls arriving in San Francisco by bus were easy targets for North Beach nightclub operators to recruit new performers. Some girls were runaways. Some just seeking adventure. Most were relocating and needed a job.

Pete and Gino sometimes sent their friend Babbalucci down to the bus station to scout for new talent. Gino let him borrow his car, and he would park in front of the station. It was hard not to notice a handsome young Italian sitting in a cherry red Cadillac convertible, wearing a beautiful custom suit and tie. The interview would be along these lines:

"Good morning," Babbalucci yells as an attractive young female trav-eler exits the bus station. "Are you looking for a job?"

"Well, yeah," is the most common reply.

"We need some dancers for our nightclub," Babbalucci states.

"Dancers? Yeah, I can dance," is a typical response.

"Well, come with me," Babbalucci says with a grin. "I've got a good job for you!"

After some discussion about the location of the club, pay, and condi-tions, many young ladies would jump into the convertible and speed off.

S ex, sex, sex! Sex was had in every corner of the club. There were no rules about sex. Once, twice, or three times a day was quite common during those wild days inside the clubs.

Sex happened upstairs, downstairs, on the stairs, on the piano, and in the tiny corner next to the jukebox. There was a mattress in the upstairs storeroom that saw a lot of action. Dark and private, it was definitely preferable to the stairs.

The women's liberation movement had been gaining momentum, especially after the publication of Betty Friedan's *The Feminine Mystique* in 1963, which had sparked a wave of feminism in the United States. The 1967 Summer of Love festivals in Golden Gate Park had awakened many to the joys of sexual freedom and experimental drugs. Contraception pills were more widely available to women, diminishing the fear of pregnancy. Women were more likely to assert their sexual desires and demand pleasurable experiences, taking advantage of their newfound sexual liberties.

Everything was changing in American society, becoming more liberal, including politics, attitudes toward sexuality and drugs, fashion, and other freedoms. The Beat/Hippie Generation threw away all the rules and had the wildest party imaginable.

Even though the hippie movement was happening throughout the City, Pete and other club operators kept their business personas, dressing in classic suits, designer shoes, ties, and dress shirts adorned with unique gold and silver cuff links.

Eventually, in the fall of 1972, the California Department of Alcoholic Beverage Control sent notices to all licensed bars featuring nude dancers that their licenses would be revoked unless the practice of bottomless performances ceased. This action followed a decision by the Supreme Court that state agencies held the right to control sexually oriented entertainment in establishments that they license. In his ruling, Supreme Court Judge William R. Rehnquist stated that prostitution, indecent exposure, and rape flourished outside California bars and nightclubs with live entertainment. The girls were ordered to cover their bottoms.

In June of 1972, Miss Doda arrived on Broadway in a chauffeured limousine and was greeted by a large crowd awaiting a very special event. She was there, along with about a dozen other topless dancers, to immortalize those mammaries that had brought her so much fortune and fame. The idea was that the topless stars should imprint in concrete various and particular parts of their anatomies, just as movie stars of yesteryear imprinted their handprints or footprints in wet concrete in the sidewalk in front of Grauman's Chinese Theater in Hollywood. Their history would be preserved forever.

Around 500 spectators, mostly male, were on hand to ogle and fantasize. About twenty women's libbers were there to protest the event and the indignity they thought it brought upon women.

(OPPOSITE) Carol plants her famous assets into wet sidewalk cement. (ABOVE) Other topless dancers after casting in front of Condor Club.

Carol was ushered through the crowd and stood apprehensively at the sloppy gray, wet, freshly poured concrete. Then she discarded the upper half of her fashionable knit pantsuit, knelt, and created her historic siliconic impressions in the sidewalk.

Afterward, she said, "It felt dirty and gritty."

Photographers snapped incessantly, recording the event for posterity. Several onlookers stated that the image resembled that of Mickey Mouse.

A thousand years from now, so the theory went, archeologists will dig up this section of sidewalk, note the impressions made thereupon, and deduce all kinds of things about our culture.

Unfortunately, the impressions in the sidewalk were eventually filled with cement as they were deemed a tripping hazard .

19

I Meet Pete

I was born in Logan, Utah, and raised in a farm family in the nearby small town of Newton. Cache Valley is an ideal location to grow up, green farmland surrounded by the gorgeous Wasatch Mountains, with the Bear River meandering through the entire valley.

Mom, Dad, and six kids occupied a small farmhouse that Daddy built; three girls slept in one bedroom and three boys slept in another. Dad worked as a truck driver at Hill Air Force Base, which was a one-and-a-half-hour drive from home. He picked up "riders" along the way to help pay the gas bill, leaving home at 5 a.m. each day and arriving back home at 5:30 p.m.

After dinner, Dad worked his 50-acre farm, raising alfalfa, wheat, and barley. The children worked all summer long, harvesting our crops and working for other farmers, picking beans and hoeing beets. On Saturdays, we all piled into Dad's car, all eight of us, and drove to Logan to shop. On Sundays, we attended church in the morning and visited uncles, aunts, and cousins in the afternoon. Mom always made a special after-church meal on Sundays, pot roast or fried chicken.

When the youngest child was old enough to attend school, Mom took a job at the Cache Valley Dairy milk-receiving room. It's where all the milk trucks drove in from the valley to unload their milk cans onto the dock. Mom stood on a metal step-up and dipped a small metal stick into each milk can as it rolled by on the conveyer belt in order to obtain a tiny sample for testing. The receiving room was ear-shatteringly noisy and open to the elements. She sometimes worked in temperatures well below zero degrees.

Cache Valley was beautiful. I received a decent education and lots of family love there—all I needed to be a successful adult—but . . . I couldn't wait to get out of there!

After graduation, I got a job as a mechanic, working in the optical department at Hill Air Force Base, repairing sextants, gun cameras, and other navigational equipment used on the F4-C jets currently being flown in Viet Nam. I worked on a bench in a warehouse with mostly men. I received the same salary as the men, $2.67 per hour. I was thrilled to make that much money. I moved to Ogden and bought my first car, a 1964 baby blue Buick Skylark.

In 1967, the family received an invitation to my cousin's upcoming wedding to be held in Sunnyvale, California. My grandmother bought me an airplane ticket to take my first flight.

I had heard and read about the wild topless shows in the North Beach area of San Francisco, and wanted to go there to experience it for myself. I had a fake ID. I located a friend who was living in San Francisco and told him I was coming out there. I practically demanded he take me to the Condor. He said he would take me to dinner and, if I insisted, to the famous Condor Club. I was crazy with excitement, wild at heart.

He took me to the City, where I had no trouble getting into the Condor. We saw Carol Doda dance on the piano, and it is quite possible that my future husband, Pete Mattioli, was there that night. I'll never know if I caught a glimpse of him or not. I didn't actually meet him until three years later.

Back at Hill AFB, they had established a new quality control program called Zero Defect. The idea was to never allow a mistake in your work at the base, as it could result in fatal consequences for one of our aviators fighting the war in Viet Nam.

Benita is crowned "Miss Zero Defects" by Major General Alan T. Bennett, commander of Ogden Air Material Area headquartered at Hill Air Force Base, Ogden, Utah

To promote the new program, they decided that a beauty contest was in order, to crown a Miss Zero Defects. She would become the base hostess at special events and promote pride in one's workmanship. My boss, Robert McFarland, entered me in the contest. I borrowed a dress, bathing suit, earrings, long white gloves, shoes, and jewelry from my roommates and entered the contest. I was completely stunned when I won! I was quite shy and unprepared for such an immense responsibility, but I assumed the role and was thrust into the limelight at the base. Of course, I had plenty of defects!

At a cocktail party at the officer's club, someone mentioned that the head of the Equal Employment Office needed a new secretary.

"Hey, Jim," he said. "You need a new secretary, right?"

Jim responded, "Yeah, my gal quit today." Looking at me, he asked, "Do you type and take shorthand?"

"Yes, of course," I replied. I had taken both classes at high school.

Jim said, "Great, you come over to the Headquarters building Monday morning. You're working for me now."

Entering my new huge office just inside the main entrance of the Headquarters Building, I saw a tall stack of discrimination claims that had been submitted by various people: women, blacks, Native Americans, and others. It was obvious that he hadn't addressed any of them, as was his job. Then I found out why.

He stared at me all day from his adjacent office, his desk positioned for the best vantage point. He kept the door open between his office and mine. Sometimes he would just hang around my desk and make small conversation. If I was standing, I would maneuver around the desk, and he would follow me. I was extremely uncomfortable while at work.

Since I rarely had much to type and he never asked me to take any shorthand, I picked up a newspaper from the man who had a small cubicle in the corner of my large office. At the bottom of the page was a small ad, which read, "UNITED AIRLINES IS HIRING STEWARDESSES. CALL THIS NUMBER FOR AN INTERVIEW."

That's it!!! I'm outta here! My ticket out of town!

I was hired by United Airlines in January 1968 and sent to Chicago for "Stew School," flight attendant training. My first base was New York's John F. Kennedy International Airport from where I worked for the next four years. Since United's routes were limited to cities within the continental United States and Hawaii, I became familiar with almost every city within their system, small cities like Moline, Illinois; Fresno, California; Allentown, Pennsylvania; and all the large cities such as Atlanta, Georgia; Seattle, Washington; and Denver, Colorado.

Hawaii was considered one of the premier vacation spots in the world and I had made a point of vacationing there as often as I could, even treating my parents to a vacation there in 1969.

In October 1970, I flew from New York to San Francisco and made the connection to Honolulu. My flight from SFO to HNL was aboard a shiny new Boeing 747 aircraft. I was lucky to snag a seat in the first class section, which included use of the upstairs lounge. In the lounge, I met a bunch of comedy writers from Los Angeles who were traveling to Honolulu to work on a proposed new TV show for Don Ho (the show finally aired in 1976). They told me they were staying at the Rainbow Tower of the Hilton Hawaiian Village Hotel in Honolulu.

I was traveling alone, as I often did. I had booked a room at the Moana Hotel on Waikiki Beach for $8 a day with my airline discount, which was half the normal price for a room at the then shabby rundown hotel. Cheap, no TV, just a radio.

The next day, I met up with my new friends from L.A. on Waikiki Beach, just in front of the Hilton Hotel. It was there I met a group of wild partiers from San Francisco, Pete Mattioli and his crowd. He was in Honolulu on vacation with several of his North Beach friends, who were out on the beach sucking up Mai Tais, playing cards, chasing women, and smoking pot under the shade umbrellas. At first, Pete paid no attention to me; he was busy playing cards. His friends kept calling me over to join them whenever I got up from my sunbathing ritual.

"Hey, come on over," they summoned. "You should meet this guy," they said, pointing at Pete.

"Why him?" I thought. Pete wasn't the type of guy I was used to dating, shorter than me and quite a bit older. Although I thought Pete was cute and kinda sexy, I wasn't particularly interested in him either, but the group was having a great time, so I joined them.

When describing our first meeting, Pete tells it like this: "She was wearing this teeny-weeny hand-crocheted bikini that barely covered the most important parts of her body, three small triangles connected by tiny strings." It was a bright orange color with a pretty white crocheted flower attached to the bra. Very 1960s.

The guys were having fun categorizing certain women on the beach after ships they knew of or had seen off the coast of Honolulu: a Sloop, Clipper, Frigate, Cruiser, Tanker—you get the idea. They called me the Destroyer, although I never figured out why.

I learned that Pete was a good friend of Don Ho, Zulu (from *Hawaii Five-O*), and some other Hawaiians in the entertainment business. When my new Los Angeles friends were finished with work, they met the San Francisco group and discovered that they knew many of the same people. We formed one big party, meeting up for dinner and hanging out on the beach.

During lunch at the beach bar, I complained about the constant sounds of Hawaiian music flowing through the hotel speakers. "I'm just sick of this Hawaiian music!" I grumbled. "Why can't they just play a little rock'n'roll once in a while?" I took my towel and marched down to the water's edge to soak in more rays. Suddenly, I heard the sounds of rock'n'roll blasting from somewhere. Pete had gone inside the hotel, purchased a transistor radio, tuned in a rock'n'roll station, turned the volume up and planted the radio in the sand next to my ear.

Well, now, he's got my *attention!* I thought. This guy is pretty cool and sure knows how to please a lady.

Later Pete told me he and his group were going marlin fishing over in Kona the next day and asked if I'd like to join them. I dumped the L.A. crowd and went fishing with the San Francisco group.

Pete and I dated on the "coast to coast shuttle" for a couple of years but weren't a solid couple until years later. He'd meet me at the arrival gate in the San Francisco or San Jose airport and carry my suitcase to the front terminal (this is before suitcase wheels were everywhere), where we would wait for his car to be retrieved by the valet service.

Off we would race to the City in his new red Mercedes 280SL convertible, hair blowing in the wind and the air full of excitement. After stops at the Condor and Roaring 20's, we'd have drinks at Vanessi's bar. Our first dinner was at Julius' Castle, a romantic little restaurant clinging to the side of Telegraph Hill. The owner greeted us like celebrities, as Pete seemed to know everyone in town. We ordered veal saltimbocca and enjoyed a bottle of Chianti Classico wine. I absorbed the dazzling San Francisco skyline from on high, and fell in love with both the City and with Pete.

In 1972, I transferred to the United Airlines domicile in San Francisco, along with my New York roommate, Shazi Ostic , another stewardess for United. We shared an apartment on Green Street for the next two years. In between my flights, I was one of many of Pete's friends who spent time at his home in Novato swimming, cooking, and horseback riding. We also spent many summer days at his second home on Bethel Island (an island in the Sacramento–San Joaquin River Delta of Contra Costa County), swimming and waterskiing behind his jet boats.

Pete told me he was looking at a property in Santa Rosa that he would like to show me. We were becoming more confident in our relationship, and he wanted me to see where he planned to build a ranch. He said it would be for breeding his champion cutting horse, Cal Bar, and training his offspring.

As we drove north, I was thinking, *Petaluma?, Cotati?* These places are hick towns and far away from the San Francisco International Airport where I worked. I had truly become a city girl.

Pete, Benita, Gino, and Gloria Del Prete, 1971.

When we arrived at the property for sale in Santa Rosa, we found a beautiful ranch-style home and a small redwood barn on the property, but the remaining 21 acres was pastureland.

Pete purchased the property and began the monumental task to build the ranch. Rich Gimondo was living with Pete in Novato and moved to Santa Rosa to help with the ranch operation, acting as manager.

Shazi moved back to her home state of New Jersey and I lived in the city with my sister-in-law's sister for a while. I soon received a frantic call from Shazi telling me that she had found my dog. "My dog?" I questioned. She said she remembered me saying that I had always wanted an Afghan Hound, and she found one running in the streets that had been on the loose for some time.

She said the dog looked like it was starving, its hair completely matted. She said she would bring her to me on a flight if I would take her. My head said no, but my heart said yes.

I met her at the airport and claimed my new dog, which looked like a large, hairless rat. I named her Keisho, a Swahili name that means "tomorrow." Maybe tomorrow she would be beautiful again. When her hair grew back in, she was absolutely gorgeous.

Benita and Pete at Grand Opening of Harrah's Lake Tahoe, 1973.

Of course, a city apartment was not a suitable home for my dog, and I asked Pete if I could keep Keisho at his home in Santa Rosa. Surprisingly, he said yes.

I began to spend more and more time at the ranch, and Pete and I became a firm couple. I moved to Santa Rosa in 1974. Pete placed a mobile home on the property for Rich, who continued on as ranch manager.

During this time, I sat through the courtroom hearings in the case of Del Prete vs. Mattioli that decided the ownership of Cal Bar, which are described later in this book. I was interested in horse ownership as well, and we became partners in a horse named San Peppy Doc.

Nine years after we met, we had planned a trip to Hawaii with Pete's daughter, Amy, to celebrate her graduation from high school. I thought how great it would be to get married on the beach where we met. I had a friend in Honolulu who told us she would make all the arrangements. Pete said he didn't think it was a good time. I was heartbroken: after nine years together, I thought it *was* time. Besides, I wanted him to travel with me and take advantage of the benefits offered by my employer.

Two years later, in 1981, we attended the Snaffle Bit Futurity horse sale in Reno. After Pete made a successful bid and purchased a mare, he turned to our friends and said, "Anybody want to go to a wedding?"

"What? Who is getting married?" our friends inquired.

"Me and Benita!" Pete told the group. I was as shocked as everyone else.

Back at Harrah's Hotel, we had a drink in the room and got ready for our wedding. I wore a black dress with plunging neckline, and a slit in the back skirt and big red roses on it. It seemed appropriate enough to me.

We smoked a joint and then left for the chapel. Exiting the hotel, Pete and I bumped into one another. "Where are you going?" I asked.

"To the chapel," he stated.

"The chapel is this way," I said, pointing towards the Truckee River.

"No, it's not, it's this way," Pete said, pointing north.

"The chapel that Joe and Nancy Scoma got married in?" I asked.

"Yes, it's this way," Pete said firmly.

"Oh, my God!" our friends were thinking. *"They are going to get into a huge argument about where the church is!"*

Turns out, I was right. I knew *exactly* where the chapel was!

When we arrived at the chapel the gray-haired ladies who ran it asked for our license.

"Our what?" I said.

"Your marriage license," they demanded.

"Well, I thought that's what you will give us," I said demurely.

"You have to get it across the street at the County offices," the lady stated, as if I was an idiot.

"Oh, OK, we'll be right back," I said.

"Better hurry, we close in fifteen minutes," she warned.

Pete took me by the hand and tugged me across Virginia Avenue, high heels clomping, and tight dress ready to split its seams, stopping traffic to get us there quickly. We ran into the courthouse and immediately felt the bright lights burning our cannabis-affected bloodshot eyes.

"Here's my ID," I told the clerk as I pulled out my driver's license.

"You don't need an ID," she stated. "What's your name?"

"No ID?" I questioned.

"Nope, just fill this out." she retorted. "And hurry, we're about to close."

Racing back across Virginia Avenue, we entered the little church.

"I'm sorry," my friend Ruth Day said. "We wanted to buy you some flowers, but there's no flowers."

"That's OK," I said.

"There's no rice, either," Nancy Scoma stated.

"That's OK, we don't need any rice," I replied.

Our group of eight shuffled around in the lobby of the chapel until one of the ladies in charge asked, "What are you waiting for?"

"Well," I said quietly. "I'm waiting for the music."

"There ain't no music!" the lady shouted.

"Oh! OK, let's go," I said, sadly. "We don't need no music, either." I naively thought there might be a canned "Here Comes the Bride" tape, but no.

My emotions surprised me and during the short ceremony, I cried uncontrollably. I didn't have a tissue on hand and when the minister told Pete he could kiss the bride, and he looked at my sloppy wet face, he didn't know if he wanted to or not. The minister ran for a box of Kleenex immediately afterward.

No pictures were taken either, as no one had a camera with a flash that worked.

I have had fun telling our wedding story to people but I remain regretful that I denied my dad the opportunity to walk me down the aisle. Luckily, he forgave me.

Pete just wanted our wedding to be *his* idea. And so it was.

Meanwhile, back at the Condor . . .

20

"This Is IT!"

One night, the music was rockin' with a topless act on stage when Gino Del Prete and Carlos Morales, who owned a topless bar called the Bunny Room, got into a drunken brawl in the upstairs men's restroom of the Condor. Before long, they pushed out the door and tumbled down the staircase, head over heels, with only the bannister keeping them from crashing onto the occupied cocktail tables. They continued the fistfight on the floor of the Condor until Pete and the doorman finally pulled them apart and threw Morales out the door.

A meeting was called, and Pete and Tony Cannistraci told Gino that they'd give him his check every week if he wanted to work a shift in the club, or they'd give him his check every week and he wouldn't work at all. Gino chose the no working option.

Gino never seemed to have enough money, and he talked Pete into loaning him $30,000 out of his end of the business. Pete asked for some kind of collateral, so Gino gave Pete some penny stock certificates that he said were worth $30,000. Reluctantly, Pete agreed to accept it and put the certificates in the safe located in the downstairs office. The only other person with the combination to the safe besides Pete was Aldo Del Prete, Gino's brother.

Pete decided they needed to replace the tables and chairs in the bar area of the club, so he asked Gino for the money he owed to pay for the furniture. Gino put him off, stalled, and made up excuses for not paying the club back. Gino followed the excuses with his usual phrase, "yaddi yaddi ya."

Pete became suspicious and had a gut feeling about the certificates. He went downstairs, unlocked the safe, and opened up the manila envelope. He found blank paper stuffed inside where the stock certificates had been.

Was it possible that Gino had talked his brother, Aldo, into opening the safe and replacing the stock certificates with paper? A huge argument ensued, and Pete demanded that Gino get the money and pay the club back within a week. Pete never found out where Gino got the money, but the entire amount was repaid by the deadline.

Pete decided he had had enough of Gino's deceitful tactics, drunken escapades, and fights. They had a buy/sell agreement in place, and since Gino had been the original owner of the Condor, the agreement stated that he had first option to buy Pete out of his interest. Gino could also sell his interest to someone else.

The next day, Pete told Gino their gig was over. He demanded Gino either buy his interest in the club or Pete would buy Gino out. Gino had first right of refusal according to the by-laws of the corporation, Del-Mat, Inc.

Gino approached several movers and shakers on the street and asked them to help him finance a buyout. He asked Jerry Morris and Ted Levine, who turned him down. He contacted Modesto Lanzone, who was a partner in Vanessi's, and Walter Keane, the artist, who was an ever-present figure on Broadway. They all turned him down.

Later that week, Jerry Morris called Pete and asked for a meeting. Jerry and Ted Levine met Pete in the Condor office and told him they would like to be partners with him. They offered to buy Gino's interest in the club. Pete worked out a deal with them, and they became 45% owners of the Condor Club. Gino was out. Pete still owned 45%, but Tony Cannistraci always sided with him, basically giving Pete controlling interest of 55%. Pete later purchased Tony's 10%, which gave him total control of any decisions at the club. Pete was delighted to be partners with two solid businessmen and guys he figured he could trust. Pete, Jerry, and Ted discussed the business daily and kept a good relationship during their partnership.

Jerry Morris was an excellent promoter, and decided the Condor also needed a new sign. He designed the now famous 40-foot tall neon sign featuring a busty bikini-clad blonde woman with flashing red lights on her nipples. Somehow, Jerry got it past the San Francisco city planners, who didn't even question the sign. The Condor owners just put it up.

In April 1970, the City of San Francisco filed a lawsuit to remove the 40-foot sign of the naughty topless lady outside the Condor. Named in the lawsuit were the owners of the building, Eda T. Moretto and John A. Chichizola, as well as the tenants and club operators, Pete Mattioli and Davey Rosenberg.

The problem wasn't that it displayed a 20-foot nudie with blinking boobs but, as Deputy City Attorney Edward J. Rothman said, the sign rose 10 feet higher than the roofline of the club, which was against city codes. The Board of Supervisors addressed this at one of their subsequent meetings, but there was never any consensus for the sign's removal. Senator Diane Feinstein, a Board of Supervisors member at the time, said that the sign "speaks for itself." Whatever she meant by that comment could be interpreted in several ways. The sign stayed up.

"This is IT! This is the place! This is where it all began! Come on in! Beautiful women and good drinks!" If you ever walked down Broadway after nine o'clock in the evening, you might have heard the voice of Art Thanish enticing passers-by to enter the Condor. Art was by far the most famous of all barkers on the street. He was very persuasive and successful at dragging almost anyone into the club; he would scream to all passing pedestrians within hearing distance.

"They only had the entrance door half open, and the doorman would stand right in front of it and check your ID like nobody's business," Art stated in a 2015 interview. "I worked at The Roaring 20's during the day and the Condor at night. Eddie Assensio was the doorman/bouncer, and Joe Cadwell worked as a bartender at night."

"Carol Doda was a total pain in the ass," Art continued. "I used to know her every move. She would go upstairs in the dressing room and come down with some kind of silk thing. If there was a young guy there, she was right on him. She didn't go with older guys at all. She fell for one of The Checkmates and dated him for a while. My nephew, Dillan, came to see me, and she took him home right away. He told me she hid his clothes when they got into bed so he couldn't run out."

"I was like Carol's father," Art confided. "When we closed the club at night, I'd go home with my wife, who worked as a stripper at the Condor. I wouldn't be home five minutes and my phone would ring. It was Carol, wanting advice. She wanted to talk about men and stuff. I'd just listen and talk to her. She had probably had a few drinks by then. She loved to drink white wine."

In 1970, Art Thanish and Jerry Morris bought a 26-foot Chris-Craft boat with a powerful inboard V8 engine. Art, a seaman and owner of The Roaring 20's, loved the water and had wanted a boat of his own. It was a beauty. Eventually he bought Jerry out of his interest and owned the boat outright. Art appropriately named his vessel *The Roaring 20's*. Bill Ahearn, who made the signs for the Condor and The Roaring 20's, painted THE ROARING 20's on the back and side of the boat, with NORTH BEACH and SAN FRANCISCO, CALIFORNIA underneath. It looked very classy.

Opening Day on the Bay, a yearly event sponsored by the Pacific Inter-Club Yacht Association, was approaching. Art decided to enter his vessel in the Opening Day Decorated Boat Parade. They would participate in the "Blessing of the Fleet" in Raccoon Straight and join the parade extending from Crissy Field to Pier 39. There was a reviewing stand and a panel of judges at the San Francisco Yacht Club. The boats would be judged as to which one was best decorated, one of several categories in the contest.

Art invited Pete to join the fun. They loaded the boat with plenty of booze and beautiful girls from The Roaring 20's and the Condor. Art sent one of the doormen down to the Salvation Army Store to buy around fifteen bras. They proceeded to "dress the ship," a practice that all ships participate in when they enter a port, flying flags on high-lines to indicate different things, such as fish caught, home port, sponsorship, etc. The North Beach crew decorated *The Roaring 20's* with one flag, then one bra, one flag, one bra, all attached along a line strung from the back of the boat to the top of the antennae and back down to the bow. Every other "flag" was a white or colorful bra.

They joined the parade and as they passed the judges stand, all the young women took off their bikini tops and twirled them over their heads, fully exposing their bosoms to the judges. Willie McCovey, a San Francisco Giants six-time All-Star baseball player, was one of the judges. He was animated with shock and laughter. His pleasure was so infectious with the other judges that *The Roaring 20's* won first place as the "Most Enlivening Entry" in the parade. It could possibly have won the best-undressed boat as well, but there was no category for that.

Art was later rewarded with a blowjob on the bow of the boat while still cruising the Bay with their award plaque safely aboard. Years later, Art commented, "We were young, dumb, and full of come!"

The boys from North Beach frequently flew down to Los Angeles to check out what was happening on the L.A. entertainment scene. They always tried to fly on PSA, the airline with the gorgeous stewardesses in colorful miniskirt uniforms.

They frequented places like Sneaky Pete's, P.J's, Whisky a Go Go, and The Factory. Pete would fly down with Gino, Coke Infante, and their friend Tommy Leggitt and checked into a local hotel. Once, after a night of heavy drinking, Pete was so hung over he could barely speak. He shared a room with Gino and was sleeping in the hotel bed when he was suddenly awakened by a beautiful, statuesque, longhaired blonde hooker. After she gently woke him, he stuttered, "Oh my God! You've gotta' be kidding me."

"Uh, uh," she replied. "What would you like me to do?"

"I can't move," Pete replied.

"Well, we'll see about that," she answered.

She began by caressing his back, his neck, and legs. With that, Pete decided he could turn over. She applied warm moist towels to his body, followed by warmed oils and creams. Pete thought, maybe this is just what he needed to cure his hangover.

She skillfully slid on top and completed what Pete thought he was incapable of doing. Then Pete heard some snickering coming from the entry door. He looked to see the three heads of his North Beach friends, stacked one on top of the other. They had hired her and had watched everything.

"You look like the fucking Three Stooges!" Pete yelled, as they all laughed hysterically.

Another time, two Cuban dancers known as the "Lollipop Twins" popped into the Condor for a cocktail one night after their performance at the Sinaloa over on Powell Street. The pretty young Latina twins were always welcomed at the club. After a few drinks, Pete and Gino invited them to Pete's apartment for a little fun. Within minutes Gino had one in Pete's bedroom and Pete had the other on the couch. Neither of the women spoke English, but that didn't seem to be a problem. A Picon Punch with champagne and a cognac float: it didn't take many of those to get a girl into bed.

After Pete's father passed away in Selma, Pete's brother, Angelo, sold the vineyard and moved back to the Bay Area. Angelo's wife, Lillian, told Angelo she wanted no part of the North Beach scene and forbid him to work in the clubs. The couple bought a home in Millbrae, and Angelo got a job working at Sunset Poultry.

After Lillian's death, Pete talked his conservative brother into buying a percentage of The Roaring 20's. Angelo managed and tended bar at The Roaring 20's, and was introduced into a whole new life. Yes, indeed, a whole new life as he began to enjoy the perks of such a job in North Beach.

One day, Joe Finocchio, who was rumored to be the biggest depositor at the Bank of America, and Angelo were talking out front of the bank with their cash deposits tucked underneath their jackets. Little did they know that the bank was being robbed as they chatted. After the thieves ran out, Angelo and Joe looked at each other, shrugged, walked into the bank, and made their deposits.

Pete and his new partners, Jerry Morris and Ted Levine, were interested in buying other businesses in North Beach, and aggressively searched out opportunities. Enrico Banducci had gone out of business at the hungry i, and opened up a bar/coffee house up on Broadway. He named it Enrico's.

As part of the purchase of Del-Mat, Inc., by Morris and Levine, they received a portion of Pete's interest in Pierre's. They purchased the famous name "hungry i" from Banducci for $10,000 and renamed Pierre's as the hungry i. It was a stroke of genius, as many tourists figured they were visiting the famous hungry i, but it was actually a topless nightclub.

The trio also purchased portions, ten to thirty percent, of The Roaring 20s, Tipsy's, and Big Al's. As part of the deal, they gained managerial rights, which they shared between the three of them. They became the topless powerhouse operators on the street.

Gino got back in business at the Expo 69 on Kearny Street, the first bar in The City to show hard-core pornographic films for drinking patrons. He was soon arrested along with manager Rene Couture, both charged with four counts of exhibiting obscene movies to the public. They both pleaded not guilty.

At the trial, a 40-minute color movie showing "unnatural sex acts" performed by three women and two men was screened for the jury in the City Hall courtroom of Municipal Judge George E. Maloney.

Pin-drop silence prevailed in the semi-darkened courthouse room throughout the unusual presentation of pictorial evidence by Inspector George J. Maloney of the Police Department's Bureau of Special Services. Codefendant Rene Couture slept through the screening of evidence.

When the lights came on again, the judge called a recess and the jurors filed out into the corridor, silent and unsmiling. The question before them when they deliberate the case was whether or not what they saw on the courtroom screen went beyond contemporary San Francisco standards.

The jury deadlocked on the charges against Gino and Rene, eight to four, with the majority voting to convict.

The case was later retried under Municipal Court Judge Leo Friedman, and on June 15, 1971, Del Prete and Couture were convicted of showing pornographic films. They were ordered to pay $1,000 and serve 120 days in jail. The charges were eventually suspended.

Simultaneously, another trial was being held in another room of the courthouse. James Mitchell, co-proprietor of the O'Farrell Theater, had been charged with showing "filthy" porno movies. They were eventually convicted as well.

❖ ❖ ❖

In 1972, Jerry Morris and Ted Levine decided they wanted to move to Denver. They sold their interest in the Condor to their friend Don Levine.

Pete was sorry to lose his good partners, but figured that he'd get along with Don just fine. Pete retained 55% of the corporation and managerial rights to all clubs within the corporation. After a few months, Pete decided to ask Don if he would like to manage the businesses. Don accepted the position.

Pete always had a desire to be in the restaurant business, so he partnered with pals Maurice Bessiere and Pee Wee Ferrari to purchase Del Vecchio's Restaurant on the corner of Montgomery and Broadway. Known as a union boss hangout and frequented by hookers, it also served up authentic Italian cuisine.

The extensive restaurant menu featured veal scaloppini, veal piccata, chicken cacciatore, ravioli, and other pasta dishes. Prime rib, steaks, hamburgers, and even Joe's Specials were available. They soon learned that the restaurant business was no piece of cake as they dealt with extensive employee theft and drunken cooks. They finally added enough salt to the cooking wine to render it undrinkable.

One day Rocky Marciano, boxing's heavyweight champion, dined at Del Vecchios while in San Francisco promoting a book that he wrote. A photo was taken of Rocky, Pete, and Freddie Apostole, another fighter. Rocky died in a plane crash the following day.

The phone rang at DelVecchio's, and Pete answered.

"This is David Chan at the Alcohol Beverage Control Department. Can I speak with Pete Mattioli?"

"Yeah, this is him," Pete replied.

"I would like you to come down to the department. We need to speak with you," Mr. Chan responded.

"What's this about?" Pete inquired.

"Just come on down. I'll let you know then," Mr. Chan replied.

Upon arriving at the ABC building, Pete was guided into a private room, where he was seated.

"We want you to do something about the hookers at DelVecchio's," Mr. Chan demanded.

"What hookers you talking about?" Pete asked.

"You know damned well what hookers. The ones sitting at your bar all night," Mr. Chan continued.

"Well, when those broads come in, I don't ask them what they do for a living," Pete explained.

"Don't give me that, Pete. You know exactly what they do for a living, and we want you to get rid of them," Mr. Chan ordered.

"Well, alright, I'll do what I can," Pete responded.

Of course, Pete knew which ladies were hookers at the restaurant. He told them, one by one, that the ABC was cracking down on them and they couldn't frequent the restaurant bar in the future. One by one, they found other establishments for their business.

As complaints from the conservative sections of the community continued to be filed, San Francisco City Hall legislators were kept busy trying to rein in activities in the North Beach entertainment establishments.

Attorney Ed Fleishell was hired by some club owners to address an anti-topless ordinance being considered by the San Francisco Board of Supervisors.

As reported by Russ Cone, the crusty "Dean of City Hall" writer for the *San Francisco Examiner* on April 14, 1970:

> Mr. Fleishell suggested four amendments to take some of the sting out of the ordinance. Fleishell secured a 7-4 approval of two of them: one preventing the police chief from closing a night spot so long as an appeal to the Board of Permit Appeals is pending, and another attempting to limit unnecessary conversation between nightclub entertainments and saloon patrons—a device to discourage B-girl activity.
>
> Supervisor Terry A. Francois carried the amendments for Fleishell on grounds that other types of licensees have the right of appeal before their operations are closed down and that the

conversation ban bordered on abridgement of Constitutional rights.

Supervisors Roger Boas, John A. Ertola, Robert Gonzales, James Mailliard, Robert Mendelsohn, and Mrs. Dorothy von Beroldingen supported Mr. Francois. Supervisors Peter Tamaras, Mrs. Dianne Feinstein, Ronald Pelosi, and John Barbagelata opposed the amendments, on the grounds they tended to weaken the ordinance, designed to control tawdry nightclub operations.

The city law enforcers seemed to be much more concerned about the Broadway barkers aggressively soliciting customers at the entrances of the clubs. They figured the barkers were far too rude and intimidating the passers-by. Later on, the city filed a lawsuit.

Meanwhile, things were getting tougher in the neighborhood. Ronnie London, a rough and tumble ex-con, owned Coffee Ron's, a coffee house and bar located on Eddy Street in San Francisco's Tenderloin district where customers were served booze in a coffee cup. London had been previously convicted of pimping in Palm Springs and on February 1, 1967, in a dispute at the after-hours Mocambo bar over ownership, Wallace "Peg Leg" Falk had shot him in the chest. Ronnie was known as a loud, rough guy who spit when he talked.

Wes Eccles, a well-known local boxer, hung around with the hard-core Tenderloin gangs. Eccles and Ronnie had some disagreement, so London sent his "boys" to work him over and teach him a lesson. They broke Eccles' arm and took out one of his eyes. The Tenderloin boys were serious about keeping control of their area.

A guy named Savage and Ronnie London wanted some of the Broadway action, and were slowly becoming more involved in North Beach businesses. They were moving in and packing iron. London went to Las Vegas with Savage, who stashed $30K cash in the trunk of his car. His car was stolen and the money was never recovered.

Another bruising tough guy, Sam Conte, owned The Loop, a cavernous building that housed a bar and a bowling alley with entrances on both

Columbus and Kearney. Conte usually came into the Condor late at night to check out the action. Pete didn't like him.

Pete worried about the seedy elements of the Tenderloin gaining a hold of businesses in North Beach. The drug scene had exploded, and some of the men were carrying guns. Pete thought that whatever he had made by then was great, but it was time to get the hell out.

"I had tried but failed to have a business association to help keep some order on the street," Pete recalls. "The other operators on the street didn't want to pay association dues or have any rules. They just wanted to take over."

Pete continued, "I'm not stupid, and could see what was going on. We had our run, so I thought I'd better get the hell out of there. Nobody would stick by me in trying to improve the street. I wanted to make the street like Bourbon Street in New Orleans. Timing is everything and I may not be the brightest guy in the world, but I can see when something is going my way and when it's not. It was time to sell."

At the same time, Pete's relationship with Don Levine had deteriorated. The San Francisco Police and Fire Departments had been citing the Condor for various incidents, and Don did not have a good relationship with them. Don ran the business differently than Pete, and Pete was often getting complaints from the police. Don and Pete argued often about the problems that arose at the clubs and Don's poor treatment of some employees.

Pete confronted Don about not unlocking the chain on the fire exit one evening just as they opened for business. Don yelled at Pete, "I run this club and I'll do things my way!"

"You run this club because I let you run this club!" Pete screamed back at him.

"Fuck you!" shouted Don.

"Fuck you!" Pete yelled back.

Pete walked over to the entrance door of the Condor and slammed it shut. He shouted to all the waitresses and bartenders to meet him at the end of the bar. Don Levine sat at the bar.

"You see him?" Pete said, pointing at Don. "He's fired! Don is fired! If he even so much as orders a drink, he pays for it. I'm running the club now. I'm your boss. Do you hear me?"

The staff huddled by the cigarette machine in the little alcove, wide eyed and stunned by what they had heard. Don wasn't very well liked with the employees anyway, so they all nodded their heads, yes.

Pete knew that Don wanted to buy the Condor, all of the Condor. Pete wanted to get out of the business, but he was well aware of the value of his operations. And, he had just signed a two-year contract with Carol Doda.

In the spring of 1974, Pete entered negotiations with Don Levine to buy him and Tony Cannistraci out of the businesses. Pete considered Don's first offer as laughable, and negotiations quickly broke off. But Pete was anxious sell and use the money to build a horse ranch in Santa Rosa. Tony wasn't excited about being a in a partnership with Don.

Pete gave Don his final offer. Don took a couple of days to consider the price, and finally agreed to Pete's terms. Pete sold his interest in the Condor and the four other clubs (Roaring 20's, Big Al's, hungry i, and Tipsy's) to his former partner, Don Levine. Don also purchased Tony's interest in the Condor, but Tony remained as bartender.

Carol Doda was still performing on the white baby grand piano.

21

Sneaky Pete's
and Cal Bar

Gino maintained his presence on the street, frequenting bars and restaurants and playing liar's dice whenever he could talk someone into it. He was still quick with that little finger flipping the dice after the shake whenever he could. Pete was glad he wasn't his partner in the Condor anymore, but they had such a deep and long-lasting relationship, they gradually became friends again.

Pete was invited to Gino and Gloria's house for dinner quite often, and they enjoyed talking about old times. Gloria prepared a long table of Italian dishes, and they often had ten or more friends for dinner. At one of these occasions, Gino mentioned that he wanted to open a bar and restaurant in a building on Lombard Street that used to house Pucci's Bar, an old hangout of the North Beach gang. He explained that due to his previous problems with the Alcoholic Beverage Control Department, they would not issue a liquor license in his name. "It's the last bar when you leave San Francisco!" Gino cried out to Pete, trying to perk his interest in becoming his partner again.

"We could name it after you, maybe call it Sneaky Pete's, like the famous club in Los Angeles," Gino continued. "We gotta do this, Pete. It'll be a goldmine. We can put your name on the license and you can manage it. I'll just bring the people, like before, and yaddi yaddi ya."

Pete was very reluctant to even go look at the old joint, let alone go into business with Gino again. But Gino convinced him that he would behave himself and didn't have any other way to make a living. Pete began to feel sorry for his old friend, and their time apart had smoothed some of the raw feelings between them.

Finally, Pete gave in and told Gino he'd go take a look.

The interior of the dilapidated building was very rundown; the old bar was still there, but would have to be refinished. Pete began calculating the costs and decided they would need additional partners and the place would require a complete remodel.

When Pete had divorced, he had purchased new furniture from one of his customers at the Condor, Jack Anderson. Jack was an independent salesperson who had a good eye for interior design. He was also a regular customer at Del Vecchio's Restaurant and sometimes frequented other North Beach establishments. Pete contacted Jack to see if he had any interest in partnering at the Lombard Street location.

Jack enthusiastically embraced the idea, but didn't have the finances to assume the remodeling costs, so he asked some of his friends in the furniture business if they wanted a share of the business. Everyone he asked absolutely wanted in on the club and soon there were six partners: Pete Mattioli, Gino Del Prete, Jack Anderson, Don Ong, Bobby Moore, and Artie Feldman. They named it Sneaky Pete's.

Pete filled out the application for the liquor license, which was quickly approved. They began working with the other partners on the interior design. An art deco look was decided on, with silver, mauve, and gray wallpaper. They replaced the worn wooden bar top with brushed stainless steel. There was room enough for a small combo to entertain between the bar and the dining room, which was in the rear of the building.

Claudio and Jaime, a popular Latin duo, was hired as the house entertainers. Smooth, sexy Bossa Nova sounds filled the room after 8 p.m. At times, local entertainers would join in to sing with the band. An excellent menu, gay waiters, and white linen tablecloths and napkins elevated the restaurant to a chic and cozy experience. Sneaky Pete's suddenly became the hottest little bar/restaurant in town, with limos often double parked in front, clogging the right lane of Lombard Street with beautiful women popping out of Mercedes sedans.

The kitchen was dual purpose. It was used to prepare the dishes, of course, but also used to hide away and snort coke. Most of the clientele was either experimenting or using coke and marijuana in those days. Lines were drawn and snorted from a plate, or even on the bar. San Francisco's elite party crowd had a new hangout.

Pete had acquired a roommate at his Novato home, a family friend from San Francisco, Rich Gimondo. Rich was a wannabe cowboy who grew up in the City and jumped at the chance to move in with Pete.

Gimondo knew of a rancher and quarter-horse breeder, Arnold Dolcini, who sold quality quarter horses at his ranch in Petaluma. They visited Dolcini, and Rich negotiated the purchase of a quarter-horse gelding, whom Pete named Arnold, and a pretty sorrel mare called Ginger. They were housed in a new six-stall metal barn Pete had erected on the two-and-a-half acre Novato property.

Pete quickly learned that horse ownership was a great incentive to attract women up to his small ranch.

"Oh, I love horses!" some of the women he met would exclaim when he told them of his two mounts.

"Can you ride?" Pete asked.

"Well, no, but I can try," would be the reply.

Pete didn't know much about riding horses either, but was determined to learn. Arnold tossed him off a few times, but Pete kept getting back on, and soon became quite an accomplished rider.

Pete's Novato house had six bedrooms, three downstairs and three upstairs. His master bedroom was large enough for two king sized beds, one a huge waterbed. There was an indoor barbeque and beautiful Spanish tiles covered the floors. The backyard featured a large swimming pool, dressing rooms, and a lovely rose garden. He didn't have a problem enticing women up to Novato for a swim, horseback ride, and lavish Italian dinners.

The neighbors entertained themselves by peeking over the fence to see if any of the ladies were topless. To their delight, some were!

Current tax laws were excellent for horse owners in the 1970s, and Gimondo explained to Pete that if he purchased a stallion, put him in training, and then bred him, he could write off most of the expenses. Of course, that meant that he would also need to buy some mares. It seemed like a good deal to Pete.

Pete purchases Cal Bar from Arnold Dolcini; trainer Larry Reeder in center.

Pete first purchased a sorrel quarter-horse stallion named Ricky Ruben and put him in cutting training with a well-known trainer who lived in Oregon. ("Cutting" is a Western-style competition in which a horse and rider demonstrate the horse's athleticism and ability to handle cattle.) He purchased some mares and sent them to the ranch to be bred to Ricky Ruben.

After a year or so, Pete began receiving reports from other horsemen who had stopped by to see Ricky, and they were not pleased with what they saw. The stalls the horses were housed in were filthy, and they were not allowed to see Ricky being ridden. Pete pulled his horse out of training with the Oregon trainer and demanded his mares be sent back to California.

Ricky Ruben missed his chance to become a futurity champion, but Pete had become hooked on cutting horses. He began to attend local cutting-horse events in Northern California.

Through conversations at these events, Gimondo learned that Arnold Dolcini had a horse named Cal Bar for sale. Cal Bar was a son of the famous Doc Bar and out of one of Dolcini's best mares, Teresa Tivio, daughter of the infamous Poco Tivio. He was quoted a price of $12,500. He told Pete about the possibility of purchasing Cal Bar.

"Twelve thousand dollars for a horse?" cried Pete when Gimondo told him about Cal Bar. "You gotta be kidding me! Ain't no horse worth that! Not to me, anyway." He dismissed any possibility of buying Cal Bar.

Seven-year-old Cal Bar was already a champion, holding several titles in working cow horse competition. He had been trained and shown by Harry Rose, a scruffy, old-style trainer who spent a good amount of time riding horses—and drinking in the local bars.

Cal Bar's accomplishments included 1970 California Reining Cow Horse Association Champion (CRCHA) Hackamore Horse, 1971 CRCHA Champion Stock Horse, 1972 CRCHA Champion Stallion, 1973 Reserve World Champion Stock Horse, and 1973 Reserve World Champion All-Around Horse. It was an impressive record by any measure. Arnold was charging $300 to breed a mare to him.

Rich talked Pete into going to see Cal Bar. When Harry Rose brought him out of the barn, Pete was smitten.

"That's one gorgeous animal," Pete exclaimed. He asked Harry to ride him.

Harry saddled up Cal Bar and entered the arena. Owner Arnold Dolcini joined them. Pete told him he liked the horse, but that $12,500 was a lot for a horse.

"Who said he was twelve thousand five hundred?" Arnold asked.

"Well, Rich here told me that was the price," Pete explained.

"I won't sell him for less than twenty-five thousand," Arnold said.

"What, are you crazy?" Pete retorted. "Now I know I'm not buying him. That's just way too much to pay for a horse."

Pete returned to his home and tended to his businesses, but couldn't get Cal Bar out of his mind. He thought about what business he might go into after the nightclub scene, which was becoming less and less attractive to him.

Rich pressed Pete to buy Cal Bar before anyone else got their hands on him. He convinced Pete that there were a lot of interested buyers looking at Cal Bar, and he had to move quickly on the purchase or lose the horse.

Pete didn't have a liquid $25,000 cash, and was trying to figure out how he could buy that beautiful horse, which he couldn't get out of his mind. He was wondering if Cal Bar could become a cutting horse after so much reining training. He asked some local trainers if they thought a champion working cow horse could compete in the cutting arena. They all told him no, that a cutting horse is a cutting horse and a working stock horse is trained differently. Pete was not convinced.

A couple of weeks passed and Pete called Dolcini.

"Let's talk about that horse," Pete told Arnold.

"Cal Bar?" Arnold asked.

"Yeah, Cal Bar," Pete confirmed. "Would you consider receiving payments for him?"

"What kind of payments?" Arnold inquired.

"How about $5,000 down and a three-year payoff for the remaining $20,000?" Pete suggested.

Arnold considered the offer. It would be beneficial to his tax situation if he didn't accept all the money in one year. He liked Pete and trusted that he would keep his end of the deal.

"Alright, Pete. Let's get the contract drawn up," Arnold said.

A few days later, both parties signed the contract and shook hands. Arnold wished Pete good luck with the horse.

When Pete arrived at Arnold's ranch to pick up his new horse he saw that Harry Rose was trying to breed him to a mare, but it was obvious that she was having none of it. She was kicking and trying to bite Cal Bar but Harry was insisting that they breed.

Pete ran over to Harry told him to give him his horse.

"What the hell are you doing? That's my horse! If you need the $300 breeding fee that bad, I'll just give it to you!" Pete screamed at Harry. "Put him in the trailer—I'm taking him now!"

Reluctantly, Harry pulled Cal Bar away from the mare and loaded him into the trailer. Pete and Rich began driving out of the ranch. Harry ran after them screaming, "Hey, where's my $300?"

"Stick it up your ass," Pete yelled out the window as they pulled out onto Red Hill Road.

Since I had grown up on a farm with horses, I was very enthusiastic about Pete purchasing Cal Bar. He put the horse into cutting training with a young trainer, Larry Reeder, who had just arrived in the area from Texas. He came to Northern California because, at the time, many of the good cutting horses were being bred there and there were a lot of horse shows. Larry jumped at the chance to compete in the California cutting arenas, but he needed the right horse to make it happen. That horse was Cal Bar.

Pete told his friends about the horse he had purchased for $25,000, and they were astounded that anyone would pay so much for a horse. Pete told them he totally believed in this horse and that Cal Bar would be a champion someday.

Gino's ears perked when he learned that there might be money to be made in the horse business. He asked Pete if he could be his partner in the horse.

"You? In the horse business?" Pete laughed.

"Yeah, why not?" Gino asked.

"Well, because I don't know much about the horse business, and you know a lot less," Pete responded.

"I know, but if you think we could make money, I'm in," Gino said.

Pete thought long and hard about partnering up with Gino again. He told Gino that he would have to come up with half the purchase price and pay half of the expenses incurred to train and show Cal Bar. Pete was thinking that it would be less of a financial burden to pay for Cal Bar's training if he had a partner, and he knew that Gino was having a hard time making money in the City. He had been in court many times, defending his showing of skin flicks at other clubs he was involved in.

Gino told Pete he was looking forward to involvement in legitimate businesses, and Pete truly felt sorry for his old buddy.

Pete was so sure that Cal Bar could become a great cutting horse that he actually gave Gino an offer he couldn't refuse. He guaranteed that if there were ever a disagreement between them and they dissolved their partnership, Pete would pay Gino the full purchase price of the horse, $25,000! It was a guarantee to Gino that he couldn't lose a dime on the deal and would actually make money if the horse didn't perform as predicted or they terminated their partnership.

The deal was made over dinner and after a few glasses of wine. When word got out of the deal with Gino, Pete's friends were stunned that he would ever agree to terms like that. But Pete and Gino had a connection from their childhood that was never totally severed, even throughout all their wild business dealings. Pete gave Gino chance after chance to clean up his act and be a good partner.

Pete's attorney drew up the contract for Gino to purchase half of Cal Bar, and they both signed it. Gino came up with half of the $5,000 down payment and gave it to Pete.

Larry Reeder and Cal Bar exploded onto the cutting horse scene, competing at several competitions throughout California and the Western states. Cal Bar won almost every show, proving time and time again what Pete had thought about him: he could become an extraordinary cutting horse champion.

With Larry Reeder as his trainer and mount, Cal Bar won both the 1974 Pacific Coast Cutting Horse Association's Open and Novice Cutting Horse Championship titles, a feat that had never been accomplished by any horse before him. As an additional trophy, he ended up fifth on the 1974 National Cutting Horse Association's Top Ten list without even trying.

Quoting Debbie O'Brien, a writer for the *Quarter Horse News*, "Cal Bar was Joe Montana, Magic Johnson, and Mozart all rolled into one. He had the brains, brilliance, and the athletic ability to do it all." Cal Bar became an instant celebrity and one of the most popular horses to breed to in his time, passing his incredible talents on to hundreds of offspring.

It was very expensive to keep Cal Bar on the road in his quest for show titles. The bills for his training and showing began rolling in, and

Trainer Larry Reeder riding champion cutting horse, Cal Bar.

Pete forwarded them to Gino, who was obligated to pay half of the costs incurred. Although Cal Bar won considerable money in the show arena, it was never enough to pay all expenses. Gino told Pete he didn't have the money, so Pete picked up the tab for thousands of dollars to keep Cal Bar on the road. Cal Bar became more valuable with every win.

22

Bad Boys

ete still owned interest in Sneaky Pete's on Lombard Street and commuted from Novato to work at the restaurant. While tending the bar at Sneaky Pete's, he began to notice two well-dressed young gentlemen who were hanging out in the club quite frequently. Sometimes they arrived in a Rolls Royce or limo, and they always spent heaps of money at the bar. Gino was immediately attracted to them and befriended them straightaway.

One of the men was named John Angelo. He usually arrived in a chauffeur-driven limousine, flashed an inch-thick stack of hundred dollar bills, a sparkling diamond pinky ring, and an expensive watch.

"He was very smooth, very cool," Gino later recalled. "Naturally, I was impressed."

Pete wasn't as impressed. Angelo was just too cocky for Pete's senses. He smelled something fishy and was uncomfortable around Johnny Angelo. Pete was more cautious in his relationship with Angelo and kept his distance from him. Turned out Johnny Angelo was working for the Federal Drug Enforcement Agency.

Pete had heard the rumors about John Angelo being a narc. He had watched as money changed hands between customers inside Sneaky

Pete's and figured that they were drug deals. He needed to be suspicious: his name was on the liquor license.

Angelo introduced Gino to a big, strong-looking kid named Bobby, who just happened to be another undercover narcotics agent.

Pete asked the other partners at Sneaky Pete's if they knew anything about John Angelo and this Bobby guy. They told him that they had met them, but they weren't worried about it. They told Pete to simmer down.

Gino and the other partners called a corporate meeting, but didn't tell Pete about it. It wasn't within the corporation rules to exclude him, and Pete was furious. He didn't know what was discussed, but later found out it was about raffle tickets to be sold at Sneaky Pete's.

Pete's brother, Angelo Mattioli, tended bar at Sneaky Pete's and kept a good eye on the place. He and Pete were close, and Angelo kept his brother informed of happenings at the club.

"A big box was delivered today, so I put it in the kitchen," Angelo said to Pete upon his arrival at the restaurant.

"What box?" Pete inquired.

Angelo said, "Well, I don't know what's in it, but it sure is heavy."

Pete went into the kitchen and cut the box open. It was full of raffle tickets. The tickets had Sneaky Pete's name printed on each one and a price of $5.00 per ticket. The grand prize was a new Cadillac.

Pete figured there was around $60,000 worth of raffle tickets in the box.

"What the hell is this?" Pete shouted. "We can't have a raffle here! It's illegal!"

Angelo agreed. When Gino arrived that evening, Pete confronted him about the raffle tickets.

"Did you order these?" Pete asked Gino.

"Yeah," Gino replied with a smile. "I've got you in for 10 percent."

"What?" Pete screamed. "We can't have a raffle here! It's illegal as hell."

"Why not?" Gino asked. "The church does it all the time."

"The church is a nonprofit organization and we're not, that's why not!" Pete yelled. "We're trying to make some money here, that's why not! And, how generous of you to cut me in for 10%! You gotta be kidding!"

Pete picked up the box, took it to his home in Novato and burned the raffle tickets in his fireplace. Gino was back to his old methods of trying to make money illegally and jeopardizing Pete at the same time.

Frustrated and worried about his name being on the liquor license, Pete marched down to the Alcoholic Beverage Control office to remove his name from the license. He was irritated that it took so long, but the license was finally changed into the name of one of the other partners.

Pete wanted out of Sneaky Pete's. The illegal raffle was the last straw. Soon afterward, Pete sold his interest in Sneaky Pete's to the remaining partners.

"Bobby and I started drinking together, cutting up," Gino recalled in an article written by Jerry Carroll and published in the June 21, 1977, *San Francisco Chronicle*. "He's a real sweetheart. We started playing golf together, lunching together shaking for drinks." The article continued:

> The friendship deepened during the next 18 months or so. On the day Del Prete's daughter was baptized, Bobby bought all the food and drink for a big party. "How much can you love a guy who does that?" Del Prete asked.
>
> Del Prete entertained Bobby with stories about the people who used to come into the Condor: Frank Sinatra, Red Skelton, Roz Russell, Walter Cronkite, Mike Connors, Clint Eastwood ("He and I are close"), Frankie Avalon, Steve McQueen, Sean Connery ("He and I are very dear friends"), and all the politicians, Jess Unruh, Phillip and John Burton, George Moscone ...
>
> "We had some of the greatest in the world come through those doors," Del Prete said proudly. He told Bobby about the bad investments, the $800,000 in stock market losses, the trouble with the IRS over $35,000 in back taxes, the lien on his home, and how the Feds even confiscated his teenage daughter's savings account.
>
> "That's rotten," Del Prete says hotly. Beyond these problems, a friend observed, "When you're used to walking around with a lot of money in your pocket and you're used to picking up tabs and all the rest, it's tough to get away from that."

Del Prete said, "I asked Bobby, what do you do? He says, 'I'm in the business. I deal.' One time he says, 'Gino, I can use some more junk. Can you get it for me? I'm not getting enough.' I told him this is not my game, but if anyone comes in, I'll put you in touch. He said he'd take care of me for doing this."

He added, "I never suspected him. Once, when a guy told me he was a cop, I said, 'You're full of s__t.'"

"So one day this guy comes into the bar and said he had some coke," Del Prete continued in the *Chronicle* interview. "I have nothing against cocaine," he said, with a graceful motion as he lifted the back of his hand to his nose, took a pretend sniff, and looked euphoric. "It's social, it's nice."

"I got Bobby a few ounces of coke." Then he said, "See if the guy can get me four or five kilos." Del Prete held his fists to his chest, emotionally. "This you have to believe in your heart. I did not believe it was heroin. I believed it was cocaine at the beginning. I don't like heroin. I don't like what it stands for," he said.

Dell Prete got in touch through an intermediary with Charles Garcia, Sr., and his son, Charles, Jr., a rock producer. The natty old man had a narcotics record dating back to 1949, and the son has proved himself a chip off the old block.

"I knew he was busted before. I didn't know it was for dope," Del Prete said. The first buy was to be two kilos worth, but a last-minute hitch dropped it to a single.

Bobby and an FBI agent posing as his backer agreed to pay $53,000 for a kilo of heroin, 12 percent pure, worth from $250,000 to $400,000. Del Prete's fee was to be $15,000, with the understanding his take could jump to $45,000 a month if business got going good.

"I would definitely have gotten out because of my feelings about heroin," Del Prete says with emphasis.

The final arrangements were made on the day of the delivery, fourteen federal agents in various disguises participated in the bust. Bobby held the door open for the agents when they rushed into Del Prete's home.

It's Del Prete's contention the federal government suckered him into getting into the narcotics trade by constantly holding out the bait of a big bonanza at a time when he was in a financial pinch.

"You could make a thief out of Jesus Christ," he said. "If somebody flaunts money at you and you need it and they keep flaunting it—it's like the Chinese water torture treatment, a drop, and a drop and a drop—pretty soon it was driving me f___ing crazy."

Observed a friend: "Poor Gino, they set him up like Humpty Dumpty on the wall. He tried to play in a fairy tale world that doesn't exist. They didn't really want Gino. They wanted the guys around him."

Said Gerald Hinckley of the Federal Organized Crime Strike Force, "Del Prete's a nice guy, really. He just picked the wrong people to go with the first time."

"He just got too greedy," said a local agent.

"Gullible," Del Prete lamented. "I'm the most gullible guy in the world."

Ever since the arrest, life has been a nightmare for Del Prete, his wife, and three children. He and the wife, Gloria, woke up at night in cold sweats and clinged to one another for comfort.

"I'm worried for the family," he said anxiously. "Claudine Longet. She takes a life and gets 30 days? If I don't get probation, there's something wrong with this system."

Oddly, he holds no grudge toward his betrayer. "Bobby? He's so pretty. There's no way you can't love him. For being so big and strong, he's humble. You know? Not a person on this earth would not love him."

"Afterward, Bobby said to me, 'Can we still play golf?' I said yes. He said, 'Are you kidding me?' I said no. When I was an altar boy, Jesus taught me to forgive everybody."

Said his wife, her eyes flashing, "He's too good. He holds no grudge against those people. He's too good. It's really killing him. That's why he drinks so much—that's all that keeps him going."

The federal Organized Crime Strike Force arrested Gino Del Prete on April 6, 1977, and charged him with drug dealing. Strike force official Gerald Hinckley said agents picked Del Prete's nightclub as the focus for their narcotics investigation because of the suspicious types seen hanging around. Among them were such reputed underworld figures as "Jimmy the Weasel" Fratianno, "Mike Rizzi" Rizzitello, and Frank "Bomp" Bompensiero, the alleged Mafia boss.

The strike force had spent more than a year on the case. Most people agreed that Del Prete was seen as a means of getting at someone known as Mr. Big. It turned out Mr. Big was Charles Garcia.

Like Del Prete, both Garcias pleaded guilty to conspiracy to distribute heroin. Mr. Hinckley recommended the judge throw the book at the Garcias but be more lenient with Del Prete.

At the trial, Gino told U.S. district Court Judge Robert Schnacke, "I'm sorry. I just made a mistake. I'm not a drug trafficker. I hope I can get probation and start all over again."

Judge Schnacke stated that he had no sympathy for Gino. He said that the ramifications of drug traffic on this scale are extremely broad, and sentenced Gino to seven years in prison.

In the July 7, 1977, *San Francisco Examiner*, Andrew Curtin writes:
NORTH BEACH FANS FLOCK TO A "GOING-IN" PARTY FOR GINO

A dapper North Beach businessman, highball in hand, surveyed the crowd jammed around the bar in the New Pisa restaurant here last night and commented.

"Well, I've heard of coming out parties. But this is the first time I've ever been at a going-in party."

He was one of more than 100 persons, most of them lifelong residents of the North Beach area, who paid $25 a head to attend a party for Gino Del Prete, 45-year-old San Francisco nightclub operator and credited with being one of the entrepreneurs who started Broadway's topless fad.

The atmosphere was festive. The guests ranged from dockworkers to longtime Broadway operators. There were hearty Latin embraces as old friends who hadn't seen each other in years exchanged greetings.

But the occasion for the party was grim—not that you'd ever guess it from the smiles, the laughter, and the cheery helloes.

Del Prete pleaded guilty in federal court here last month to charges of conspiracy to distribute heroin, and was sentenced to seven years in prison by U.S. District Judge Robert Schnacke.

He has until a week from today to surrender to the U.S. marshal's office.

"I don't want to talk about it," he said last night as he accepted the hugs and handshakes of well-wishers.

"Look, this is my life that's on the line. I've got enough heat already. I don't need any more."

David Brown, one of his attorneys who also was among the party guests, also declined to discuss the case.

"There's nothing to say at this time," he said. "Maybe later. Comment now is inadvisable."

Del Prete waived a hand at the assembled crowd.

"Look at these people," he said. "These are the people I grew up with. They know me. They're my friends. They know I wouldn't do what they (the federal prosecutors) said I did."

New Pisa proprietor Dante Benedetti was in the kitchen, putting the final touches on the evening's meal.

Del Prete stepped outside for a moment.

"The smoke's getting to my eyes," he said.

"Look—maybe someday I can tell the whole story. But not now. I don't want any publicity.

"Let's just forget about it for tonight, OK?"

Notably absent was Pete Mattioli.

From his jail cell at McNeil Island Corrections Center, Washington State's version of Alcatraz, Gino filed an appeal on the grounds that Judge Schnacke had improperly advised him about his possible sentence when accepting the guilty plea. The appellate court voided the plea and sentence, and he was released after four months. Bail was set at $100,000.

At his second trial in July, 1978, a federal jury convicted Gino of selling two pounds of heroin and five ounces of cocaine. He faced a prison term of up to 90 years and a maximum fine of $150,000, according to the prosecutor, Mark Webb. Gino was immediately remanded to jail over the objections of his attorney, Robert Kissel.

Gino ended up serving less than five years in prison.

While Gino was in prison, Pete called his attorney to activate the contract that he had signed with Gino for the purchase of Cal Bar. He had to come up with $25,000 cash to satisfy the terms of the contract. Gino had only paid a fraction of the expenses associated with Cal Bar's training and trips to compete in the show arena.

Pete began to put together the cash to buy him out. Gino countersued, saying that since Cal Bar now had so many championship titles, he must be worth more than a million dollars. Gino sued Pete for $1,000,000, stating that that was his value now.

Pete knew he needed to retain the best counsel in the business to get him out of this jam. He hired a prominent San Francisco trial attorney, Charles O. Morgan.

At the trial for ownership of Cal Bar, Gino's wife, Gloria, sat alone during the proceedings. It didn't help her case any that her husband couldn't be there. He was sitting in federal prison with a narcotics conviction.

Mr. Morgan presented evidence furnished by Pete that showed he had financed all but a fraction of the expenses incurred by Cal Bar's training and showing career. Gloria, unfortunately, could not produce documentation showing that Gino had kept up his end of the agreement.

Pete won the case easily, although it cost him thousands of dollars in attorney fees, not to mention the $25,000 he still needed to come up with to buy his horse back.

Pete sold his beautiful cherry red Spectra 20 ocean-racing boat and his summer home at Bethel Island, ten miles east of Antioch, California, to finance the buyout. His relationship with Gino was finished. They never spoke again.

23

NIGHT THREE:
The Mysterious Death
of Jimmy the Beard

Acalamity occurred at the Condor on November 23, 1983, long after Pete sold the club. Don Benson was the owner at the time. The bouncer/manager, Jimmy the Beard, was found dead, crushed between the ceiling and the piano after it had risen to the top, a stripper, still alive, next to him, having survived the night. In 2015, I interviewed Art Thanish, a seaman who occasionally worked at the Condor, and the one who discovered the tragic scene.

"As my real job, I was a seaman. I shipped out all over the world on the *SS Lurline, SS Mariposa*, and the *SS Monterrey*. All three ships belonged to Matson Lines and were home-ported in San Francisco. I belonged to the Seaman's Union of the Pacific, commonly known as the SUP.

"Don Benson bought the Condor from Don Levine. He hired Jimmy Ferrozzo (aka, Jimmy the Beard and Jimmy Vento) as doorman, bouncer, and sometime manager. But when Don went out of town, he asked me to take care of the bank. I was still working at the shipyard, so I asked Benson why he didn't have any of his partners do the banking. 'Well, I can't trust them,' was his answer.

"So, I would go to the Condor at 3 a.m., switch the banks, and go to work at Hunter's Point. When I got to the Condor the morning of

Jimmy's death, I couldn't get in. The door was dead-bolted from the inside. I thought, 'Well, I guess the janitor must be downstairs in the office cleaning or upstairs in the dressing rooms cleaning.' So, I thought I'd come back later, after lunch.

"When I arrived at the shipyard, I got to thinking about it, and thought something is not right. I told my boss, 'I'm leaving now and I'll tell you about it when I get back.' I went to the Condor, and the door was locked. I'm the one who caved it in."

BENITA: "You did?"

"Yes, it was just a chicken-shit deadbolt. A little brass bolt. And I got in.

"I could hear a girl yelling. I looked and saw a girl on the piano up on the ceiling and she is yelling, 'Get me out of here!'

"And I said, 'Don't worry. I'm coming.'

"I could see Jimmy's legs, hanging out over the edge. I knew it was him because I could see his cowboy boots, but I didn't know he was dead. So I said, 'Wait a second. I'll lower the piano down.' I went over to the breaker and boom, nothing. So I went over to the panel, click, click—and nothing. I went upstairs and into the dressing room. I crawled through the tunnel leading to the piano.

"When I got there, I grabbed ahold of Jimmy and realized he was dead. Oh, no! Jesus Christ! Jimmy's dead!

"See, Jimmy was so big, he didn't press the limit switch, and it just suffocated him. The girl was smaller, so it left her enough room to breathe. They weren't on top of each other. No, in fact, his face was right in her muff! Yes, I swear to God! He was right in there! He was fully clothed and she was naked. He was right in the Y!

"Jimmy must have hit the switch with his boot.

"'Get me out of here!' she's yelling at me.

"I went back down and called 911. I saw her purse on the bar, all the cocaine and shit. So, I snorted all the cocaine that was on the bar and took the purse down to the office. I didn't want that to get into play."

BENITA: "Were there other drugs around, or did it look like there was a fight?"

"I really can't say. I honestly don't remember that."

BENITA: "Lucky Lucchesi told us that there were broken chairs and glass all over the club. He said it looked like a hurricane blew through. He thought there had been a big fight."

"I don't know about that."

"When Joyce Shank came to interview me at my home, my wife and I were just sitting there, smoking weed, drinking, and doing everything wrong.

"The doorbell rings and [a woman] said, 'Joyce Shank. Channel 7 News. Can I talk to you?'

"So I said OK and boom, the floodlights came on. They got me right there. They asked to come in, and I let them in.

"I gave the interview and they showed it on the Channel 7 News that night."

The following is a transcript of the news report, which appeared on Channel 7 News on the day Jimmy died. Pete Wilson was the news anchor for the show, and Joyce Shank interviewed Art Thanish at his home.

PETE WILSON: "Bizarre! Perhaps the most overused word on television newscasts, but how else to describe the death of Jimmy the Beard? How else but—bizarre. Bit by careful regarded bit we are learning more tonight. Joyce Shank with more on that sleazy story from that seamy part of town."

JOYCE SHANK: "The lights may be on, but the Condor Club is sealed tight. [*photo of coroner's* CLOSED *sticker*] The County Coroner's sticker. Homicide investigates the bizarre death of this man, James "The Beard" Ferrozzo. Found at ten this morning on top of a piano suspended in the air, almost flush with the ceiling, he was fully clothed. Next to him naked, but still alive, was 23-year-old Teresa Hill."

ART THANISH: "I went in the club and saw James Ferrozzo and this girl pinned to the ceiling with the piano. I heard the girl's voice, so I went through the dressing room and through a tunnel where Carol Doda goes to do her show, and saw that the girl was alive. And I reached down and felt Jimmy, and, well, I knew he was dead."

HOMICIDE INVESTIGATOR MARTIN DEAN: "There were things thrown all over the place, broken glasses, broken mirrors, and so on. Once we are satisfied as to how that was caused, then we'll determine what to do."

JOYCE SHANK: "There was blood found at the scene; homicide tells me only one wound was found. The girl's wrist was cut. The pair had been drinking and maybe indulging in other drugs from midnight on.

"The piano is used by Carol Doda and others as a stage entrance coming down from the ceiling, but apparently last night, it went up with two apparently inebriated people on top. How did it get going?"

ART THANISH: "There is a small ladder that goes to the piano, and at the top rung of that ladder there is a switch with three buttons: UP, PAUSE, and LOWER. And it could have been kicked by a foot, and, I don't know, but it could have happened."

JOYCE SHANK: "Sources say James the Beard, a big man, over 6 feet, 220 pounds, saved the young girl's life. He was so large that his size gave her the two inches of breathing space she needed to survive the crush."

SUZIE (DANCER): "Even if you are loaded, you would have to know...you'd have enough time to know when the ceiling was coming."

JOYCE SHANK: "But the man who died, James "The Beard" Ferrozzo, was face down when he was found. Chances are, he never saw the ceiling coming. The survivor, Teresa Hill, is at home tonight, incoherent when found; says she remembers nothing of what happened. Autopsy results will be completed by noon tomorrow. And drug and alcohol blood level tests will not be final until next week."

PETE WILSON: "Blood, broken glass, a lot of broken furniture. Apparently a struggle of some kind beforehand. But not necessarily directly involved in this, right?"

JOYCE SHANK: "I don't know yet, that's why there is an investigation going on. They did wind up together on the piano."

PETE WILSON: "The curious thing, we were talking about this morning, the curious thing is the assumption that you would know that piano was going up. If you are that drunk, you might well not know."

JOYCE SHANK: "Precisely. Plus if someone would try to murder one or two of those people, wouldn't they have to wait a long time for the piano to go up?"

PETE WILSON: "I don't know."

Joe Cadwell, longtime Condor employee who was the bartender the night Jimmy lost his life, recalls Jimmy Ferrozzo:

"One day, Jimmy came in the Condor. He popped into the Condor quite often, sometimes with a young, longhaired blonde beauty. Jimmy picked up a girl at the bar and took her to a hotel where she said she was staying. I think it was one of the big hotels on the hill. He used to like to pick up girls and throw them over his shoulder, you know, like he was kidnapping her.

"He went up to the hotel, and one door opened behind him and one door opened in front of him. Out came two guys with lead pipes. The girl had set him up. They beat the hell out of him. Jimmy had a huge neck, and fought back hard. He went down on his knees but somehow got out of there.

"He came into the Condor with a big hole in his head, so I poured a bottle of vodka over the wound to kill the germs. He said it was Tommy Hunt and someone else in Ronnie London's group from the Tenderloin who beat him. Joe said that Tommy Hunt had come in the Condor prior to the beating and showed Joe a gun. Gangs and guns had become a part of the North Beach scene by that time.

"I said, 'You don't need that.'

"'Yeah, I do. I need it to kill all the germs around here,' was Tommy's reply.

Recalling the tragic night, "I locked him in there," says Joe. "Art Thanish found him because he came in through the subterranean basement of the building the next morning."

The next day, Joe gave his deposition to the San Francisco Police Department.

Pete also knew Jimmy quite well; his was a familiar face on the street, having worked at several establishments as bouncer and manager. He was a big, tough-looking bear of a guy, but a wide smile gleamed through his thick dark beard.

Most people on the street knew you didn't want to mess with Jimmy. He had thrown many drunks out of the places he worked, and it was quite possible someone was seeking revenge to even the score.

After the incident at the hotel on the hill, Pete told Jimmy, "You've got to have eyes in the back of your head, Jimmy. You need to be careful."

"For how long?" Jimmy asked.

"For forever," Pete replied.

After Pete moved to Santa Rosa, he remained friends with Jimmy until his death. Jimmy often rode his Harley up to the ranch, usually with a pretty longhaired blonde in tow. He loved to visit and check out the horses. Jimmy was a happy guy, his huge grin flashing through his hairy bearded face and mass of long unruly hair. He was tattooed, and dressed in leathers and cowboy boots, rough and unkempt looking. Some of the cowboys around the ranch wondered who the heck he was. Pete often had to "explain" some of his old North Beach friends to the conservative horse people he dealt with at the ranch. But most of these friendships from the City have endured throughout Pete's life, no matter what these people looked like.

No one knows the true circumstances of Jimmy's death except Teresa Hill, the lady who was with him when he suffocated on the top of the famous white piano. She refuses to speak about the matter to this day.

Jimmy (The Beard) Ferrozzo talking to Pete on Broadway.

24

Whatever
Happened to ...?

DAVEY ROSENBERG Davey Rosenberg continued to add Broadway entertainment club owners to his list of clients and at one time represented eleven venues as their booking agent.

He was constantly dreaming up schemes to draw attention to Broadway. He once chained Yvonne d'Angers to the Golden Gate Bridge when she was threatened with deportation. He led a Ban-the-Bra Movement on lower Market Street. He loved helping his new hires in selecting their show biz names: Nude Orphan Fannie, Shelley Knockers, Thoroughly Naked Millie. He sent several topless girls on a commuter flight to Los Angeles where they were promptly arrested upon arrival. Davey was quoted as saying, "A good press agent has a fantasy mind."

During the early 1980s, Davey returned to help his father manage his newsstand-bookstore, Harold's, at Taylor and Post Streets. Davey suffered from the debilitating effects of diabetes during his final years. Big Davey Rosenberg, the self-described "World's Greatest Press Agent," passed away on September 17, 1986, due to an apparent heart attack. He was 49 years old.

GINO DEL PRETE After Gino was released from prison, he separated from his wife, Gloria. Carolyn Del Curto Infante, his friend and the ex-wife of Coke Infante, was his companion during the later years of his life. He spent his final years at her home in Rutherford, California, making wine and olive oil, and enjoying the country life. Carolyn preceded Gino in death, passing away July 13, 2017. Gino passed away on March 21, 2018, with his family by his side.

Carol performed into her 70s.

CAROL DODA In 1968, at the height of her fame, she was profiled by Tom Wolfe in an essay, "The Put-Together Girl," in his book *The Pump House Gang*. The book's introduction proclaimed, "She blew up her breasts with emulsified silicone, the main ingredient in Silly Putty, and became the greatest resource of the San Francisco tourist industry."

During the '70s, Miss Doda became a spokesmodel for KGSC, San Jose television Channel 36, appearing in commercials promoting "The Perfect 36." Her slinky voice intoning, "This is Carol Doda, and you are watching the Perfect 36," was the bait for late-night TV viewers during commercial breaks. Although her San Francisco landmarks were not "Perfect 36s," rather humongous 44s, that didn't seem to matter to her fans.

In 1975, her famous breasts were cast in dental plaster, which was to be auctioned as the "booby prize" at a benefit for the Women's Board of the San Francisco Museum of Art. A bronze and gold loving cup was made from the mold and awarded for the "Dumbest Car" in the first Artists' Soap Box Derby.

Doda worked as a stripper until 1985, performing at the Condor three nights a week up to the age of 48. Her costume, usually a gold lamé dress accented by elbow-length gloves, was slowly removed during her shows until she just wore a G-string and tiny wrap skirt.

Carol continued to improve her other entertainment skills as well, taking more vocal lessons from Judy Davis, acting lessons from Herbert Ball of ACT, and dance lessons from choreographer Dotti Lester. She got healthful tips from her pal Jack LaLanne, a fitness guru and proprietor of health centers. "I used to sound like Andy Devine," she once confided. "Now? I don't think I could compare my voice with anyone." Carol performed at several venues throughout California and Nevada, including Harrah's Tahoe. She tried desperately to change her image and create a show that included music, dancing, and humor, performing fully clothed at most of these out of town venues to emphasize the fact that she really was legitimate. Carol also sang, fully clothed, with a rock band she formed, the Lucky Stiffs, who performed cabaret style in several North Beach bars.

Carol made several acting appearances in the 1980s—adult feature films like *Honky Tonk Nights*, where she wrote and sang the theme song as well; mainstream movies like *Head*, which was produced and written by Jack Nicholson and Bob Rafelson and starred the Monkees; and made several appearances on the TV series *Nash Bridges*—but a successful acting career continued to elude her.

She opened Carol Doda's Champagne and Lace Lingerie Boutique on Union Street, where she sold upscale women's lingerie. She loved the business, and once said that some of her best customers were transvestites.

Carol performed cabaret style until 2009 at several San Francisco venues, including Amante, Tupelo, and Enrico's Supper Club. Two of her favorite songs to perform were "All of Me" and "That Old Black Magic." She was available for certain publicity gigs, and once was the guest of honor at a special VIP party held by Steve Wozniak of Apple Computer fame, at which she did not perform.

Carol, who was born in 1937, maintained she had never married, but at a young age had given birth to two children with whom she had little contact since: a daughter, Donna Smith Terzian, who predeceased her, and a son, Tom Smith.

Doda passed away on November 9, 2015, from kidney failure. She was 78 years old. A well-attended public service was held at the Tupelo Club, where she sometimes performed, on Grant Street in San Francisco. Those who knew her warmly memorialized her.

THE CONDOR Pete sold to his 55% of the Condor to Don Levine in 1974. Don continued to operate the club with topless entertainment, which included Carol Doda's performances. Later on, Levine sold to Don Benson, who owned the club when Jimmy "the Beard" Ferrozzo suffocated on top of the famous piano in 1983.

Topless dancing at the Condor ended on New Year's Eve in 1987 and was replaced by a Barbary Coast revue that celebrated life in San Francisco after the 1849 Gold Rush. The new image at the Condor failed miserably.

Soon afterward, the Condor sat abandoned and deteriorating for over two years. Walter Pastore assumed ownership of the Condor in 1990 and spent more than $200,000 restoring the club. Pastore took down the famous sign depicting Carol Doda with blinking boobs, cut it in half, and attached the upper half to the wall inside the entrance of the club. In its place, he erected an art deco neon sign, which simply reads CONDOR. In small lettering at the bottom of the sign it says TOPLESS A GO-GO. The Condor operated as a sports bar and grill from 2005 to 2007.

Presently, an American company, Déjà Vu, Inc., headquartered in Las Vegas, Nevada, and operated by Harry Mohney, owns the Condor. Déjà Vu operates over 130 strip clubs in 41 states, as well as multiple clubs in Europe, Australia, Canada, and Mexico. The company also operates a large chain of adult retail stores, multiple online adult enterprises, gay bars, nightclubs, and has substantial real estate holdings. The clubs typically aim for a clean and upscale atmosphere, and offer fully nude or topless stage dancing as well as lap dances. Déjà Vu sponsors many sporting events such as charity golf outings, speedboat racing, and off-road truck racing.

On June 19, 2014, the Condor hosted a huge soirée to celebrate the fiftieth anniversary of the first topless performance by Carol Doda at the club. The Mistress of Ceremonies was burlesque dancer Kitty Chow. The two Italian-American partners who owned it in 1964, Pete Mattioli and Gino Del Prete, spoke at the event. Carol Doda did not attend, but was represented by D'Arcy Drollinger, a drag queen, dressed as Carol in a gold lamé gown, blonde wig, and her oversized 44-inch bust.

Still operating as "The Condor, San Francisco's Original Gentlemen's Club," the tiny neighborhood jukebox bar has gone through many transitions. It has earned a prominent place in San Francisco entertainment history, and certainly deserves to keep it.

THE CONDOR SIGN The original Condor sign was of a completely nude blonde figure (Carol Doda) with blinking red lights on her boobs. That version was only up for a couple of months and received so many complaints that the San Francisco Supervisors demanded a bra and a bikini bottom be painted onto the image. Pete obliged, and had a black bikini painted over the lady's offending parts. The flashing lightbulbs remained.

The red-light-nippled marquee dominated the corner of Columbus and Broadway for twenty years. In 1991, when Walter Pastore purchased the club, he wanted to put more of an emphasis on it as an Italian-style bar-café and less on topless entertainment. He desired to create a museum inside the club, including the sign and historic photos of the Topless Revolution that began there.

The sign was taken down and cut in half. Its removal attracted a large crowd of onlookers, watching to see if the worker's fingers lingered a few extra minutes on the red light bulbs before removing them. He removed the lights in quick haste, depriving the onlookers of any undue titillation, so to speak.

The top half, complete with flashing light boobs, is a prominent feature inside the entrance of the Condor to this day.

Taking down the iconic Condor sign.

Benita and Pete with Star, a gelding by their champion cutting horse, Cal Bar.

PETE AND BENITA Pete couldn't stay out of the restaurant/night-club business for long, and in 1976 he purchased a lunch/bar business in Santa Rosa called the Music Box. He booked rock'n'roll bands for a couple of years, but when disco came in vogue, I convinced him to change the format to disco. The club was wildly successful, with lines out the entrance on many occasions. It became a regular hangout of the Oakland Raiders, who stopped by after bed check to party with Santa Rosa's prettiest women. Pete and I became friends with several of the Raider stars, including Ken Stabler, Ted Hendricks, Dave Casper, Jim Plunkett, and coaches Tom Flores and Sam Bogosian. On many occasions, team members stopped by the ranch after practice to remove their tape and down a few beers.

I continued my flying career with United Airlines, so it seemed like much of my life was on the road. I'd unpack from a working trip to Beijing or London and repack my suitcase to attend a horse show in Fort Worth.

We named the ranch Double Bar M Ranch. For the next sixteen years, we operated as a private breeding and training ranch, breeding as many as 125 horses in one season. The ranch became what would be called a "Stallion Station," where we offered to complete breeding services for other stallion owners. In addition to quarter horses, we stood champion thoroughbreds such as Cari County and Macho Hombre.

Cal Bar passed away in 1990 at age 24 after complications from surgery to remove an enterolith, an intestinal stone. Since we wanted to continue ranching, we accepted our first boarded horses in 1990 and transformed the breeding ranch to a boarding ranch, adding arenas and other amenities requested by boarders. We are proud to have helped several young trainers begin and develop successful businesses in Sonoma County. To appeal to a more diverse equestrian community in Sonoma County, we changed the name of our ranch to Hunter Lane Equestrian Center in 2014 and promoted English as well as Western disciplines.

We retired when we sold the Equestrian Center in 2017, and continue to live in beautiful Sonoma County. I'm still amazed that Pete was able to transform his life from being one North Beach's most dynamic nightclub owners to being one of the North Bay's most successful horsemen. We were honored to receive the 2013 Excellence in the Horse Industry Award given by the Sonoma County Fair Board. The Sonoma County Horse Council presented us with the prestigious 2016 Equus Award for our achievements in the local horse community. More recently, in 2018, Pete received the Founders Award for his work in the establishment of the Sonoma County Horse Council.

In September of 2018, NBC's *Bay Area Revelations* produced a historical documentary titled "Sexual Revolutionaries." The production focused on the men and women throughout the San Francisco Bay Area who have contributed to the liberalization of sexual freedoms throughout the history of San Francisco.

Pete Mattioli, Carol Doda, and the Condor were featured,

Pete with Darci, a transvestite who portrayed Carol Doda at the Condor's 50th Anniversary party, June 19, 2014.

a segment of which related to the sixteen years that Pete was a partner in the club. Pete was interviewed for several excerpts of the film. With candid humor, he spoke about his time at the club, the celebrities who frequented the Condor, and, of course, Carol. He shared some amusing stories and addressed the evolving freedoms of erotic entertainment in the North Beach area throughout the time of his ownership of the Condor from 1958 through 1974. The documentary also addressed the liberalization of the LGBTQ communities, the women's liberation movement, porn shops and shows, and sexual toy sales. The documentary can be viewed online at www.nbcbayarea.com/on-air/as-seen-on/Bay-Area-Revelations-Sexual-Revolutionaries-Full-Episode-494858731.html.

The wine stains remain on Pete's birth certificate to this day, and he still shines his shoes with polish stored in the old apple crate. My hand-crocheted orange bathing suit with the little white flower rests peacefully in my dresser drawer, silently keeping so many more secrets.

Pete and Benita, 2012.

Acknowledgments

My ten-year journey to complete this book would never have come to fruition without the encouragement and support of so many people. Night after night, usually at the dinner table, I listened to stories told by my husband, Pete, and his many friends who shared this journey with him. I was constantly thinking, somebody has just got to write these stories down. As time went on, it occurred to me that I might just be the only person who knew or had known so many of the characters in this book. Even though I have never written a book, it became more and more apparent that I was the one to document Pete's integral part of North Beach's history.

Much of the history in this book took place before I met Pete in 1970. I relied on the memories of the many people I personally interviewed that were part of the North Beach scene at the time, and used their stories here. I researched the archives of the *San Francisco Chronicle, San Francisco Examiner*, and the *News-Call Bulletin* for information that I could not obtain from people I was able to interview. The excellent writings of the reporters employed by those newspapers, and quoted in this book, gave me excellent documentation of some of the happenings during the 1960s and the 1970s.

First, of course, I'd like to thank Pete for the beautiful life we have shared and always being there for me when times were tough. We've worked together in all aspects of the businesses we owned in Santa Rosa, including the Music Box, For Pete's Sake!, the Double Bar M Ranch, and the Hunter Lane Equestrian Center. It's our extraordinary love for each other that got us through life's most challenging phases, and I can honestly say he listened to me, heard my voice, and always let me be me.

In 1978, I decided to open a teen dance club in downtown Santa Rosa, a desire I had always held after complaining there was "nothing to do" when I was a teen. I called it Fourth Street Annex and reproduced a street scene décor inside the club. Pete knew it was a long shot that I would make money, but he did all he could to help me build and manage the club. I discovered that it's difficult to make enough money to cover operating costs by charging a four-dollar entrance charge and seventy-five-cent soft drinks. He knew that, but supported me anyway. Two years after opening I had to sell the dance club and tackle a very large loss. We agreed that it was a good lesson in running a business, and we moved on.

Pete's generosity is quite amazing, lavishing me with clothing, jewelry, and flowers on all special occasions. I began to fly the international routes for United Airlines in 1986, and when I returned home, Pete never failed to have a beautiful bouquet of flowers waiting for me. Sometimes there would be four or five arrangements he had placed throughout the house to welcome me home. He always makes me feel so very special. It's been a fabulous ride whether it was in his little red Mercedes 280SL convertible, on a champion cutting horse named Cal Bar, or in Harrah's private jet. Pete has fulfilled my every dream.

I'd like to thank my first cheerleader, Marlene Cullen, founder of Writers Forum in Petaluma, California. Her passion for helping new writers—in particular, me—was very inspirational. It was at one of Marlene's workshops that I met Rayne Wolfe, who handed me a card stating that she was a writing coach. That's it, I thought. I need a coach! Rayne spent countless hours working with me and encouraging me to carry on.

When I met my editor, Mark Burstein, I knew I'd hit the jackpot. A native San Franciscan, he was very interested in Pete's story and has been there for me at every turn. As an exceedingly accomplished author and editor, he brought his deep experience and professional editorial guidance, which was exactly what I needed to reach publication. His encouraging words were so appreciated. His patience and tolerance for my slow writing pace was endless.

My talented book designer, Barbara Genetin, was a pleasure to work with as she laid out the book, placing stories and photos where they made the most sense. Thank you, Barbara.

I give gratitude to my friend Lynn Newton for her excellent work in designing my book cover, with attention to the tiniest detail. She shared a long-held secret with me that when she was young, she actually purchased one of the famous topless swimsuits, just because she just "had to have one." Unfortunately, she was too shy to ever wear it.

I greatly appreciate the support of Pete's friends Art Thanish, Joe Cadwell, Danny Kanights, Tony Cannistracci, and Frank Alioto for consenting to interviews with me. These guys provided firsthand knowledge of their North Beach experiences, and allowed me to tell the story based on their many observations.

The excitement and encouragement I've received from many friends has given me inspiration to complete the book. Thank you to my friend Michael Harkins, author of *Move to Fire*, for his assistance and support. I owe special gratitude to our friends Hope and Jack Nisson, Elizabeth Palmer, Vivien Rowe, Rosemary Petersen, Sarah Bozich, Rafael Delgado, Christy and Ron McClean, Carolyn Burgess, Olivia Dudley, Christine Campbell, Mike Cetraro, Armando Garcia, Michelle and Glen Lau, Jan White, Patty Aguirre, Chris Wall, Mark Marshall, Sahar and Joel Bartlett, Betty Bessiere, John Lombardi, Mario Lombardi, Carmella and Oddie Hoffman, Joan and Phil Priolo, Lisa Thomas, Mark Calcagne, and Bess Cadwell for listening to these stories, eyes wide open and with positive words: "Can't wait to read the book!" They kept me going.

None of this could have been written without the encouragement and unwavering love I've received from my family. Special thanks to Kathy and Steve Christensen, Bruce Christensen, Glen Christensen, Barbara Wood, Cheryl Mattioli, Leanna McAllister, Kevin Buford, Elaine Loosigian, Cyndi Hill, Kim and Greg Loosigian, Rik and Amy Withington, and Takoda Withington. I am especially grateful to my mother, Phyllis Christensen Clarke, an accomplished poet in her own right, for her encouragement, sweet love, and the devotion that only a mother can give.

Printed in the USA
CPSIA information can be obtained
at www.ICGtesting.com
LVHW010721130524
779829LV00009B/189

9 780578 416670